THE
SOUTHERN ELECTRIC
STORY

THE
SOUTHERN ELECTRIC
STORY

A personal celebration of
'the world's largest main line electric railway'

Michael H. C. Baker

Foreword by Chris Green, Managing Director, British Rail InterCity

Silver Link Publishing Ltd

To John and Andrea, whose hospitality
helped make this book possible.

© Michael H. C. Baker 1993

First published in March 1993

British Library Cataloguing in Publication Data

Baker, Michael
    Southern Electric Story: Personal Celebration of
    the World's Largest Electric Railway
    I. Title
    385.0942

ISBN 0 947971 85 8
Silver Link Publishing Ltd
Unit 5
Home Farm Close
Church Street
Wadenhoe
Peterborough PE8 5TE
Tel/fax (08015) 4-4-0

Printed and bound in Great Britain

The third rail - a Ramsgate to Charing Cross train approaching Ashford, 9 November 1991.

CONTENTS

It is a tribute to the skill, dedication and vision of its engineers that the story of Southern Electric is still able to fascinate and excite so many people, among whose number I am proud to include myself.

It is easy to look back on the past as a 'golden age' in the Southern Electric story, but as Michael Baker admirably demonstrates, the present and the future have an equal lustre. From 1986 to 1991 I had the honour of developing Network SouthEast, which inherited the mantle of responsibility for the Southern Region. These were years of unprecedented growth, as employment in and around London boomed. They also saw the start of a dramatic new chapter in the story told here: the opening of the cross-London Thameslink line, the launch of the

Class '442' 'Wessex Electrics' and - our proudest moment - the development of the revolutionary 'Networker' train for the South East.

One are of the development of our railways that is often overlooked is the contribution made by people. For it is only through the dedication of the drivers, guards, signalling engineers, station managers and countless others, that the technological and engineering achievements of the past 60 years have any meaning. Now, as the railways move forward into a new era, one thing is certain - that without their efforts the Southern Electric story could never have been written.

Chris Green
Managing Director, InterCity

Below **Chris Green at York with the first 'Networker' to be handed over to Network SouthEast.** *BR*

Left Southern Electric, past, present and future - Waterloo International, 20 July 1992.

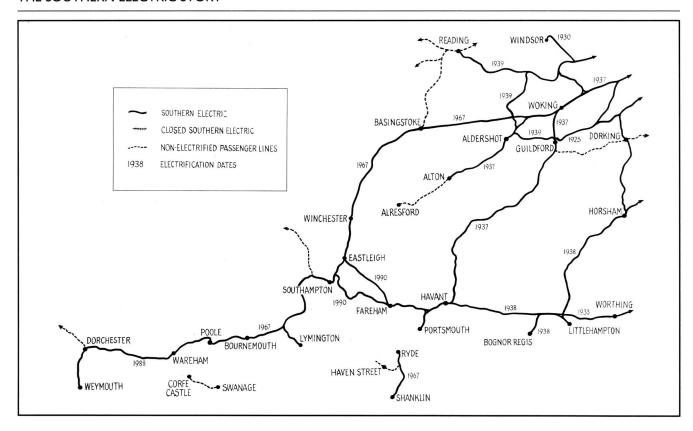

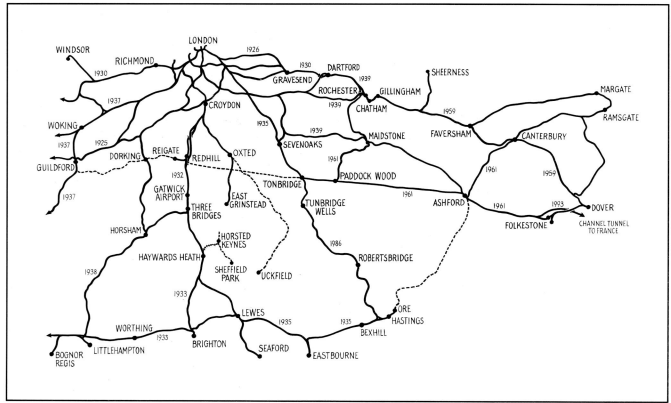

The Southern Electric system. *Christina Siviter*

INTRODUCTION

January 1993 marked the 60th anniversary of the inauguration of the Brighton line electrification, the first all-electric passenger main line in the country. Since then the process of electrifying all of the Southern network beyond the suburban area, from the Medway towns around the Kent, Sussex, Hampshire and Dorset coasts to Weymouth has proceeded more or less continuously, broken only by the war years and the subsequent period of recovery. This book is a celebration in words and pictures of those 60 years.

I was giving a talk to the Shropshire Railway Society once (yes, I know it's a long way from things Southern) on the Brighton line and the Chairman remarked that the Southern Electric was a 'no-nonsense working railway'. He was exactly right. It took me a very long time to realise that this railway, upon which I was brought up and which I know better than all other railways, was not the dull, unglamorous but necessary drudge I had supposed, but was actually a thing, if not quite of beauty, then of vast and complex fascination.

Enthusiasts tend to enthuse over locomotives, steam first of all then, failing that, diesel and electric. Multiple units have not traditionally caused hearts to beat faster. In my case there was little logic in this for I thought that trams, which in essence are single unit electric multiple units, were the bees knees. My friend Barry pointed out the flaw in my philosophy some 40 odd years ago when we were both pupils at Whitgift Middle School in Croydon, a town with a bewildering network of electric railways. He, like Cecil J. Allen, had travelled in Switzerland and had been won over. Both argued that what was good enough for scaling the Alps was surely adequate for the conquest of the North Downs and Grosvenor Bank. It took me a long time to see it.

The customers, who mattered rather more, had no such inhibitions. Not surprisingly they much preferred the clean, frequent and punctual electric services. It is surely no coincidence that far fewer stations have been closed on the Southern Electric than any other section of the British railway system. Despite the occasional hiccup Southern Electric has always been able to look to the future with confidence. Dwindling traffic, diminishing returns and the threat of closures are to all intents and purposes miseries outside its experience.

Electricity may always have been the propulsive power of the future but the multiple units upon which the Southern has relied for 60 years have not always been the most up-to-date of vehicles. The Southern believes in good housekeeping and does not throw its money around; it does not lightly dispose of anything, and has a tradition of re-using all that is re-usable. This is certainly part of its fascination. Like their suburban precursors, many of the EMUs which inaugurated stopping services along the Sussex coast in the 1930s were converted from pre-Grouping steam-hauled carriages. Ever since then new bodies have been stuck on top of old underframes (if you keep your eyes peeled you may yet see the initials LSWR on an EPB axlebox), steam stock has been refurbished, motors have been re-used, interiors have been gutted and rebuilt, so that whenever 'new' trains appear, one can never be quite sure just how new is new.

Gradually the enthusiast fraternity is catching up with the general public and today the pitying, deprecatory howl 'It's only a multiple unit', in which I confess I used to join, is heard less often on the platform ends at Clapham Junction, Eastleigh, Tonbridge and elsewhere.

For this much credit must be given to the Southern Electric Group. Founded on 20 May 1970 in order to ensure that something of 'the historic rolling-stock steadily disappearing on the Southern shall be preserved for posterity', it has not only achieved this, but has also chronicled month by month in its *Live Rail* the fascinating and ever-changing story of 'the world's largest electric railway'.

Looming mightily just over the horizon is the Channel Tunnel. The timid, mealy-mouthed prevarications of the Thatcher years notwithstanding, this promises to be the greatest opportunity offered to our railway system this century. If Southern Electric is allowed and has the vision to grasp what is on offer, one may hope that the new millennium will inaugurate a golden era of rail travel outstripping any within living memory.

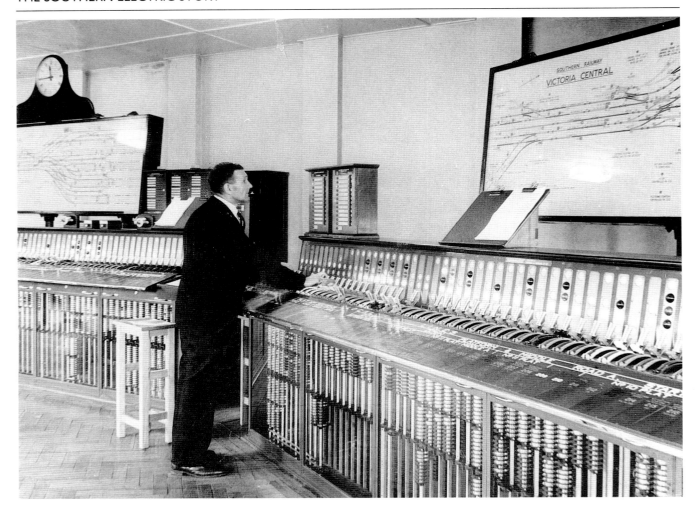

The notion of electrifying the main line from London to Brighton had been around for many years, but not many people know that it is Winston Churchill we have to thank for finally making it possible. More of that anon, but in the meantime, whilst young Winston was recovering from his experiences during the Boer War and getting elected as MP for Oldham, a proposal for an entirely new line was put forward in the autumn of 1901 by the London & Brighton Electric Railway Company.

Revolutionary in concept, there would be no intermediate stations and it was stated that the 48-mile journey would be covered in 32 minutes. Splendid though this would have been - picture with what joy a 'Wessex Electric' or a Class '91'-propelled rake of Mark 4s would greet such a race track - the great scheme never left the drawing-board. The opposition of the London, Brighton & South Coast Railway, the necessity to serve such intermediate generators of passengers and income as Croydon, Redhill and Haywards Heath with branch lines, and the absence of the technology to guarantee success, all brought about its downfall.

Considerably loopier was the suggestion of a monorail, put forward in 1902; it would be several generations later that the truth would dawn that nothing can compete with the ordinary railway for its flexibility, simplicity, safety record and high speed potential.

A good deal more worrying for the LB&SCR was the success of the electric tram in the London suburbs, and in 1903 powers were taken out to electrify the entire Brighton system, both suburban and long distance. Electric trains began to operate publicly on the alternating current 6,600-volt system over the South London line between London Bridge and Victoria on 1 December 1909. It was an instant success and work shortly began on extending the overhead wires down the main line as far as Coulsdon. The electrical equipment was made in Germany. Taking absolutely no account of this whatsoever, a Serbian student assassinated the Archduke Ferdinand and his wife in Sarajevo; within a month the First World War had begun, and the LB&SCR's grand electrification works ground to a halt. Work did not restart until 1922, and was completed by the Southern Railway on 1 April 1925.

Reappear centre stage Winston Churchill. In 1924, having moved from the Liberal to the Conservative party, Churchill was appointed Chancellor of the Exchequer by the Prime Minister, Stanley Baldwin. In 1929 he found himself faced with the horrendous problems brought about by the Wall Street Crash. One measure designed to ease unemployment was the abolition of railway passenger duty. It didn't save the Government, which lost the General Election held on 30 May 1929, but the Southern Railway found itself £2 million better off.

A condition of the abolition of the duty was that the money gained should be used for capital works, so in 1930 the SR announced that it would electrify its main line south from Coulsdon to Brighton; included would be the coast line eastwards as far as Worthing. The total cost, which would include electrifying 162 track miles, new rolling-stock, resignalling south of Coulsdon and alteration of a number of stations, notably Haywards Heath (which was completely rebuilt) and Brighton, was estimated at some £2³/₄ million. £500,000 worth of equipment had been ordered before the year was out.

In the meantime the Brighton company's overhead system had been steadily dismantled in favour of the third rail, and the last overhead train worked from Victoria to Coulsdon North on 22 September 1929. The advantage of the 600-volt direct current third rail system, introduced by the London & South Western Railway in 1916, was that it was cheaper to install and to maintain. It was not, however, so well suited to long-distance travel, but clearly two systems could not operate on one not very large railway, so all future Southern extensions would be third rail.

Work went steadily ahead. The hub of the new system was at Three Bridges where a control building was erected, overseeing the current supplied from an enlarged Deptford power station and from the National Grid, transformed down from 33,000 volts to 660 and sent out by way of 18 substations. Nearly 13,000 tons of third rail and 50¹/₂ route miles of supply cables were laid. Three-aspect colour light signalling replaced semaphores south of Coulsdon on the Quarry line (although semaphores were still to be seen in profusion at Redhill into the 1970s), automatic signals and track circuiting was introduced,

Above left **The all-electric signal box at Victoria Central.** *National Railway Museum, York*

Left **4LAV No 2926 pauses at Redhill on its way from London Bridge to Brighton. In the distance one of the 1940-built 4LAVs is at the up platform, whilst opposite is an LSWR '700' Class 0-6-0 on a Guildford train.** *National Railway Museum, York*

and 24 signal boxes were done away with leaving 15, only six of which worked all round the clock. One all-electric box at Brighton did the work formerly allocated to six mechanical ones.

The first section, as far south as Three Bridges, was inaugurated on 17 July 1932.

Passengers could now for the first time board electric trains at Coulsdon South, Merstham, Redhill, Reigate (on the Guildford line), Earlswood, Salfords, Horley, Gatwick, and Three Bridges. It says something both about the popularity of the new trains and the density of the population in these parts that all the stations are still open and doing excellent business. This entire length was served by quadruple tracks; the Quarry line, opened to bypass the Redhill bottleneck and problems with the South Eastern & Chatham Railway in 1900, passed through Coulsdon North and avoided Coulsdon South, Merstham and Redhill.

It is of interest that the 1 mile 83 chains of the Redhill to Guildford cross-country line as far as Reigate was also electrified. Reigate was much the older settlement; indeed, the original station at Redhill was known as Reigate, but by 1930 the former had grown greatly, the twin towns were joined together by bricks and mortar and tarmac, and both generated much income for the railway.

Not very much notice was taken by the local press - the completion to Brighton would be a different matter - but the *Brighton Evening Argus* of Saturday 16 July noted, alongside a much fuller report of the half-yearly meeting of the Brighton District of the Manchester Unity of the Independent Order of Oddfellows, that

The first train to Three Bridges will leave Victoria at 6.55 am arriving at Three Bridges at 8.24 am. In the up direction the first electric train will leave Three Bridges at 7.6 am, Reigate 7.20 am, arriving at London Bridge 8.5 am (change at East Croydon for Victoria, arriving at 8.26 am). On weekdays the service will consist of two trains per hour, one serving Victoria and the other London Bridge, but extra services will be introduced during the morning and evening rush periods to cope with the extra traffic. With the opening of this further extension, all the stations between Coulsdon and Three Bridges will virtually be included in the Southern Railway's suburban area, and will

have the benefit of greatly increased cheap ticket facilities (single fare for the double journey). A number of additional stations outside the electrified area, to which steam train services will run from Three Bridges, are included in the cheap ticket arrangements. This part of Sussex is very popular with ramblers at weekends.

The trains which worked this initial section of Britain's first electric main line were the units which would faithfully serve it for the next 35 years, trundling up and down, stopping at all stations countless times, day in, day out. They were very much what one would have expected, a development of the suburban units of 1925 with a nod in the direction of Maunsell's contemporary steam-hauled main-line stock. Each unit was made up of four carriages, one more than the suburban EMUs, and there were initially 33 units. Coded 4LAV, this didn't mean that each unit could boast four lavatories. Far from it. It meant that there were four carriages in each unit and that two lavatories were available to a select few passengers. These select few, 30 1st and 24 3rd Class, were the ones who found seats in the trailer corridor composite. The other 40 1st and 180 3rd Class passengers sat in non-corridor vehicles and had to cross their legs.

By the time I came to travel regularly in the 4LAVs, after the Second World War, most of the non-corridor trailer 1st compartments had been downgraded to 3rd (later 2nd) and these, with their deep cushions and ample leg-room, were what the cognoscenti headed for. Wider than the 3SUBs, except at the brake ends where they were pinched in as on contemporary steam stock, they were dignified-looking vehicles. The design of the motor coach fronts closely followed that of the suburban units with windows set on either side of the route number stencil. This was usually either a '12' (Victoria-Brighton semi-fast), a '13' (London Bridge-Brighton semi-fast), '14' (Victoria-Brighton slow), '15' (London Bridge-Brighton slow), '34' (Victoria-Reigate), or '37' (London Bridge-Reigate). Numbered 1920-53, 40 units were ordered but only 33 were built, it being decided that a cheaper option would be to have two coach units of converted steam stock for stopping trains between Brighton and Worthing. In late 1936 the 4LAVs had 1000 added to their numbers.

2 Electrics to Brighton: 1933

As well as the suburban stock, the express units were also under construction, and trials took place before the official inauguration of 'Britain's first all-electric passenger main line' on 1 January 1933. Not surprisingly this momentous event captured the imagination of the press. The *Brighton Daily News* of Saturday 31 December 1932 published a picture spread marking the 'inauguration yesterday' of what was clearly a publicity run. Various dignitaries including the Lord Mayor of London are shown standing at Brighton station, most puzzlingly in front of what would seem to be the Canterbury & Whitstable's preserved *Invicta* built by Robert Stephenson - was it brought from Canterbury especially for the event? There is also a picture of one of the express units arriving at Worthing station on what was obviously a miserably wet day, and below it is shown 'the Shoreham medallion . . . specially struck to commemorate the electrification'.

The next day, 1 January, it was the turn of the general public.

Unwonted quiet reigned at Brighton station - even for Sunday. Trains were arriving from and leaving for London - four to the hour each way - but they were electric trains which slid quietly in and out of the station. Gone for ever, so far as passenger traffic on this section of the line is concerned, are the puffing and panting steam locomotives that used to rumble in with their human freight.

On Monday evening the *Argus*, between the card for the Manchester races and 'wireless programmes for tonight', reported that

Before addressing the Grand Jury at Brighton Quarter Sessions this morning, the Recorder, Mr J. D. Cassels, KC, MP, said he did not as a rule select that occasion for making observations outside the business of the Court, but he would like to congratulate that ever-advancing Borough upon the introduction of a service of electric trains between the greatest Metropolis in the world and the best British coastal resort.

A fine, unbiased judgement which must have left the assembled cat burglars, vagrants and loiterers with intent somewhat nonplussed.

Twenty-three six car units were built for the express services between Victoria and London Bridge and Brighton and Worthing. Three of the trailer carriages in each unit, a 3rd and two composites, were very similar to current steam stock, being wooden framed with

steel panelling, and were built at Eastleigh and Lancing. A Pullman car was incorporated in each unit, hence the codename '6PUL'.

Pullmans had long been associated with the Brighton line, more so than any other, and the Company's works was situated at Preston Park in the Brighton suburbs beside the main line. Each car weighed 43 tons, was equipped with a kitchen, and seated 12 1st and 16 3rd Class passengers, getting on for $1\frac{1}{2}$ tons of carriage per passenger, but comfort and luxury was what Pullman travel was all about. The cars were all-metal and were built by Metro-Cammells.

The motor coaches were even more massive vehicles, weighing 59 tons. Built by the Birmingham Carriage & Wagon Co and Metro-Cammells to R. E. L. Maunsell's designs, they also had all-steel bodies. Of saloon layout, they seated 56 3rd Class passengers in addition to the guard's van and driver's cab. The front of the latter followed standard Southern Railway practice. Wider than either that of the suburban or the 4LAVs, with its confident curves and bold profile it was a fine piece of design and was not to be rivalled until the 'Wessex Electrics' arrived more than 50 years later.

Each unit developed 1,800 hp and its stated maximum speed was 75 mph - which was certainly exceeded on occasions. Three units, Nos 2041-3, were designed to work the 'City Limited', the crack businessmen's express between London Bridge and Brighton, and they were all 1st Class, except for the motor coaches.

Lovers Walk, the carriage depot to the west of the main line immediately beyond the junction with the Lewes line, and south of the Pullman works at Preston Park, became the electric train depot. Brighton's steam shed, however, continued in business; steam still had a monopoly of goods traffic and there were plenty of steam-hauled passenger trains operating east and west and along the branches to Steyning and Horsham, and from Lewes to East Grinstead and Tunbridge Wells, whilst through summer holiday trains from the Midlands and elsewhere were still worked down the main line by steam.

Thus no great slaughter of steam locomotives followed the Brighton line electrification. The last of the celebrated 'Gladstones' went in 1933, but the first had gone 23 years earlier. *Gladstone* himself was preserved by the Stephenson Locomotive Society in 1927 and put on display in York Museum - it would be 64 years before he would be seen in Brighton again.

The very last main-line steam working between Victoria and Brighton, the 12.05 am from Victoria on 1 January 1933, was hauled by 'Baltic' tank No 329 *Stephenson*. The seven engines of this class then moved to Eastbourne shed, but with electrification looming there the 4-6-4Ts were taken into Eastleigh Works in 1934-5 and converted to 4-6-0s, in which form they ran on the Western Section until the early 1950s. The more modern 'King Arthurs' and 'Schools' moved elsewhere, although the latter class was often seen at Brighton right down to the 1960s. The other big Brighton tanks, the 4-6-2s and 4-4-2s, found secondary work for another 20 years, whilst the ill-fated Maunsell 'River' 2-6-4Ts were converted to 2-6-0s after the Sevenoaks derailment, and thenceforward were to be seen all over the Southern.

Two 'Gladstone' 'B1' Class 0-4-2s, Nos B172 and B197, at Brighton on 8 March 1921. *O. J. Morris*

3 The years of transition: 1933-37

The way it was. One of the magnificent Lawson Billinton 'Baltic' tanks, No 332 of 1922, then brand new, gets a grip on the crack London to Brighton business-man's express, the 5.0 pm 'City Limited' out of London Bridge, on Brockley bank. The carriages are Marsh semi-corridor 'balloon' stock, built especially for this service; the fifth vehicle is a 12-wheeled clerestory-roofed Pullman from the late 1890s. *Author's collection*

A Marsh 'H2' 'Atlantic', No 425 of 1912, with the down 'Southern Belle' in Southern Railway days. *Author's collection*

The big LB&SCR-built passenger loco-motives were never displaced from the principal express workings on the Brighton line as long as steam remained in charge, but they were augmented by Southern Railway 'N15' 'King Arthur' Class 4-6-0s. No 803 *Sir Harry le Fise Lake* is seen here with the small six-wheeled tender with which all this batch were paired in order that they could fit on the smaller Brighton line turntables. *Author's collection*

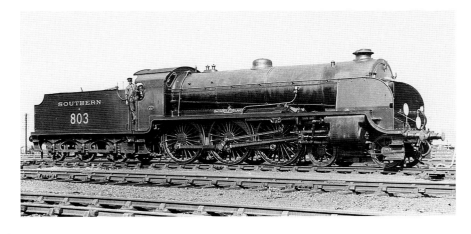

LB&SCR-designed overhead electrics and Southern Railway third rail units alongside each other in the sidings at Coulsdon North in September 1929 at the time of change-over to the third rail. The motor van of the Brighton unit (left) is the third vehicle; the third-rail unit is converted from LSWR-built steam stock. *H. C. Casserley*

The very last overhead electric about to leave Victoria for Coulsdon North shortly after midnight on Sunday 22 September 1929; leaning out of the cab window is driver Bill Mann of Coulsdon. One can see how little thought had gone into the appearance of the original Brighton line electrics - merely two windows cut into the flat carriage end with a primitive route indicator stuck between them. *Author's collection*

It was as well that the Southern Railway based the design of its EMUs on the vastly more handsome LSWR units. One such, No 1212, stands at West Worthing alongside another LSWR migrant, 'T9' No 336, on a stopping service from Brighton on 17 April 1933. *Madgwick collection, Brighton Libraries*

A 4LAV unit, No 2946, heads through the South Downs at Patcham with the 2.14 pm London Bridge to Brighton stopping service in British Railways days. *John Scrace*

The prototype main-line express motor car, No 11001, shortly after completion at the works of the Birmingham Railway Carriage & Wagon Co in 1932. This massive vehicle weighed 57 tons and seated 56 3rd Class passengers in two saloons as well as accommodating the guard, the luggage over which he watched, and the motorman. *Colin Marsden collection*

Motor car No 11037 at the head of 6PUL unit No 2019 with a mustachioed motorman starring vigilantly ahead. The main visual difference between this and the prototype was that it had a conventional curved bodyside, a feature which gave it a rather neater appearance; the luggage van was also enlarged and the seating capacity reduced to 52. Production of the 45 vehicles was shared between Birmingham RC&W and Metro-Cammells.

Although No 11001 bears the number of the original unit, 2001, it became part of No 2041, one of the three 'City Limited' sets, with all-1st accommodation in the trailers. In 1937 the 6PUL and 6CIT units were renumbered 3001-37 and 3041-3.

The style of lining out - left over from the days of elaborately-panelled wooden-bodied stock - varies slightly between the two vehicles, and was something of an anachronism on modern all-steel electrically-propelled carriages; it disappeared during the war years. Nevertheless one 6PUL motor car managed to retain full pre-war lining throughout the war years and into the first months of Nationalisation. *Colin Marsden collection*

The world's first all-Pullman electric multiple unit at Victoria about to set off for Brighton in January 1933; 3rd Class motor car No 89 is the leading vehicle. Each five-car unit was powered by eight BTH 225 hp traction motors which enabled it to keep to the 60-minute non-stop schedule with ease. There were three five-car 'Belle' units and a further 23 composite cars for the 6PUL and 6CIT units, making 38 cars in all. They were all-steel vehicles constructed by Metro-Cammells, and although built entirely within the Pullman tradition they introduced certain innovations, notably the slight slope inwards from the waist to cantrail and all-electric cooking.

So famous did the name 'Brighton Belle' become that it is easily forgotten that for its first 18 months of operation the old steam days title of 'Southern Belle' was carried. Miss Mary Hardy, the Mayor of Brighton, performed the renaming ceremony in June 1934. *Author's collection*

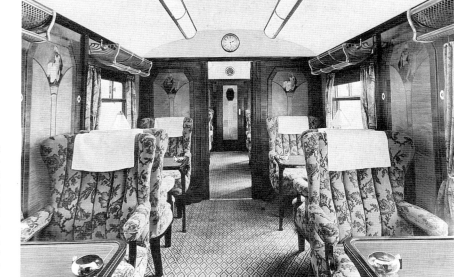

The interior of a 'Brighton Belle' 1st Class Pullman. The marquetry was particularly fine and little expense was spared to ensure maximum luxury during a journey which was scarcely longer than some outer London commuters endured in vastly less electrified splendour. There is the hint of a clerestory in the roof, although nothing of it showed in the smooth steel exterior. *Colin Marsden collection*

A contemporary Southern Railway poster. *National Railway Museum, York*

The Hastings and Eastbourne lines were the next to be electrified. The old order is represented by 'H1' 'Atlantic' No 2037 *Selsey Bill* passing Norwood Junction with a London Bridge to Eastbourne express composed of modern Maunsell corridor stock a few days before the electrics took over on 7 July 1936. *Author's collection*

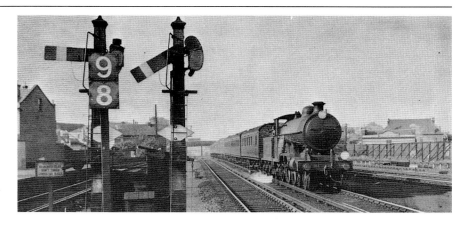

Two 6PAN units on a London Bridge to Eastbourne express working near Purley Oaks before the Second World War, but after renumbering into the 3021-37 series; the two lower-quadrant LB&SCR-built signals are a reminder that semaphores were to be found in abundance in the first decades of electrification, and even now, in the 1990s, they have not quite vanished, as we shall see later. The PAN motor coaches were almost identical to the PUL units but, as on contemporary steam stock, sliding ventilators in the windows replaced louvres and droplights. The result was a most handsome-looking carriage.

The interiors were also well appointed, with lots of varnished wood and deep cushions, but, alas, the riding was not of the same high standard. The weighty PUL and PAN motor coaches gave the track a real thumping and each thump transmitted itself to the passengers, augmented with sundry jerks and shudders. There was nothing unsafe about this, but they certainly were not as comfortable as they looked. Instead of a Pullman, refreshments in the 6PANs were provided in what the Southern Railway was pleased to call a 'pantry car' - hence the unit's title - which elsewhere would have been a 'buffet'; this was staffed by a Pullman attendant. Although the PANs were built for the Eastbourne and Hastings scheme, it soon became regular practice to run a PUL and a PAN unit together on all the principal Sussex coast express workings between Littlehampton, Worthing, Brighton, Seaford, Eastbourne, Hastings and London. *Author's collection*

Contemporary with the 6PANs was a new type of main-line unit for stopping and semi-fast services. This was the 2BIL, and No 2054 is seen bringing up the rear of a Brighton to Victoria stopping train at Hassocks in July 1967. Alongside are trailer cars from withdrawn 6PANs.

An official English Electric photograph of four 2BILs (with a 4COR in the far distance attempting vainly to hide behind the semaphore signal) when new. No fewer than 152 2BILs were built between 1935 and 1939 and they became a familiar sight all over the Southern Electric system between Portsmouth and Hastings and on stopping and semi-fast services out of Waterloo, Victoria and London Bridge (Brighton side). BIL meant bi-lavatory; the SR assumed that all its passengers were up on their Latin and understood that 'bi' meant two - one lavatory in each carriage. As can be seen, both coaches had corridors but there was no gangway connection between the two. The motor coach also accommodated the guard's van and 48 3rd Class passengers in seven compartments; in the trailer coach there were four 1st Class compartments seating 24 passengers and four and a half 3rd Class ones with 36 seats. To my mind the BILs were the handsomest of all the Southern Railway EMUs, but you can make up your mind for yourself for happily one unit, No 2090, has been preserved as part of the National Collection. The bodies were wooden framed with steel panelling. *Colin Marsden collection*

The first ten 2BILs, originally Nos 1891-1900, differed in several respects from the rest, and three of them are seen here at Polegate after withdrawal in 1969. The windows did not fit as flush to the carriage sides, the droplights were wooden framed, and there were louvres over the doors (the middle coach has been transferred from a later unit). The guard's van was slightly smaller, allowing seven rather than six and a half compartments. The all-electric control gear was cab-mounted, while on the remainder of the BILs it was electro-pneumatic, underframe-mounted. In 1937 the 2BILs were renumbered, so they eventually ran from 2001 to 2152.

2BIL No 1897 glistening in ex-works condition. *National Railway Museum, York*

The very last BIL, No 2152, equally pristine, and seen from the corridor side, reveals many of the differences. *National Railway Museum, York*

The earliest stopping services along the Sussex coast after electrification were provided by suburban units, namely the original LSWR three-coach 3SUBs of 1915 (see the upper photograph on page 17) until purpose-built, or rather rebuilt, units were ready. These were the 2NOLs, and NOL, with the Southern Railway's lavatory fixation, meant no lavatory at all, so tough luck. All 196 vehicles had begun as LSWR non-corridor steam stock in the early 1900s; they were given new underframes and, of course, electrical equipment, but as far as the passengers were concerned they were distinctly mature by the mid-1930s. Numbered 1813-90 each unit seated 130 3rd Class and 24 1st Class passengers. No 1815 leads a 2BIL at Polegate on a Brighton to Eastbourne, Hastings and Ore service. *Author's collection*

So we arrive at what have become probably the best known of all the Southern Railway main-line electrics, the 4CORs. Until now each electrification scheme had involved former LB&SCR routes; now it was the turn of a former LSWR main line, the direct route through Woking, Guildford and Petersfield to Portsmouth. Work began in the summer of 1935, trial runs to Portsmouth were operating by April 1937, public running of the new electrics began before the official inauguration, notably for the Coronation Spithead Review by King George VI on 19 May, then on 4 July full electric services between Waterloo and Portsmouth Harbour were inaugurated.

For the expresses a new unit was needed. The earlier six-car PULs and PANs had proved generally satisfactory but the battleship-like construction of their motor coaches was giving the track a terrible pounding, whilst their riding qualities left a good deal to be desired. In addition, the lack of a gangway connection between units was an inconvenience.

Thus the Portsmouth units were given gangwayed front ends, with a rather small driver's cab to one side of the gangway and the headcode stencil on the other. This one-eyed look, plus their association with Portsmouth, earned them the almost inevitable nickname of 'Nelsons', although to we trainspotters at Clapham Junction they were always known as 'belly-wobblers' on account of the bounce of the leading corridor connection as the carriage leaned through the curves of the fast lines. The layout of the motor coaches, and the appearance from the side, was similar to the 6PANs, but their construction was quite different, being of lighter wooden framing with steel panelling. If not beautiful, the 'Nelsons' exuded character.

As with the previous schemes, the Portsmouth electrification was a great success. The *Portsmouth Evening News* recorded that

> The number of services will be increased from by 100% to 157% with accelerated journey times varying from 5 to 56 minutes, and giving an average acceleration of 9 minutes.

More 2BILS were built for the slow and semi-fast Portsmouth line trains. Two units forming an up slow are seen at Farncombe on 19 May 1937. *Box collection, National Railway Museum, York*

Coincidental with the inauguration of the electric services a new paddle steamer, the *Ryde*, built by Dennys of Dumbarton, was introduced on the Portsmouth-Ryde run. In 1936 the Southern Railway carried 2,326,259 passengers on this route, 'nine times the population of Portsmouth and an increase of 50% over the number carried in 1926'. No fewer than seven steamers were employed on the Portsmouth-Ryde run; a sign of changing times was the increase in cars carried between Portsmouth and the Island, up from 4,000 in 1926 to nearly 22,000 in 1936. A generous spread of eight pictures, including one of the PS *Ryde*, commemorated the official first run. The *Ryde* is seen here when new. She is still existence, holed up as a floating restaurant on the Medina in the Isle of Wight; there are plans to restore her to working order. *Colin Caddy*

Expresses ran every hour, calling at Guildford and Haslemere, and took 94 minutes; on Saturdays, the *Evening News* proclaimed

> . . . there will be four fast corridor trains per hour to cope with the holiday traffic to Portsmouth, Southsea and the Isle of Wight.

Amongst the passengers on the inaugural Portsmouth electric were the Southern Railway's General Manager, Sir Herbert Walker, and an assortment of Lord Mayors, ordinary mayors, civic dignitaries and an Admiral of the Fleet. They arrived

> . . . in one of the newest trains which are being built at the company's own workshops at Eastleigh and Lancing. On these trains the compartments are decorated in the harmonious and distinctive form. The first class restaurant car is a composite saloon and ordinary compartment vehicle. The third class restaurant car is a combined dining and kitchen car.

Elsewhere in the paper another glimpse of the rigid class divisions still prevalent in Britain in the 1930s is given in a sad little list of the four passengers killed in an accident at Swanley Junction. The occupations of three are given: one was an aeronautical engineer, one 'a servant from Edenbridge', the third 'a parlour maid from South Kensington'.

At the celebratory luncheon to mark the Portsmouth electrification, Sir Herbert Cayzer, a Portsmouth MP, allowed himself a pat on the back because he 'had voted for the Government which guaranteed the capital, principal and interest, and that had helped the Company to go forward with their scheme more quickly'. The SR Chairman, Mr R. Holland-Martin, wasn't going to let him get away with this. In responding to the toast he noted that 'This was only the first part of the scheme. About a year from now they would be ready with . . . an alternative route to London and they would be able to go by electric train from Portsmouth to Hastings.' To give Sir Herbert his due, he did state that since 1923 the Southern Railway 'had spent £16,000,000 on electrification'.

The officially preserved motor car from unit No 3131 is seen restored to original condition at the May 1988 Woking Open Day. It will be noted that lining had not entirely disappeared. The lighter construction of the motor cars and the fact that each unit was made up of only four carriages instead of six enabled the Southern Railway to equip each unit with two rather than four 450 hp motors.

The Portsmouth electrification brought the third rail 25 miles down the Western Section main line to Woking. The preserved 2BIL No 2090 is seen in Woking station in May 1988.

A 12-coach express headed by 4COR No 3112 speeds through the rich rural landscape south-west of Haslemere where Surrey, Hampshire and Sussex meet, on 27 June 1937. Alfred Lord Tennyson lived hereabouts; he looked out of this window and wrote: 'You came and looked, and loved the view, Long known and loved by me. Green Sussex fading into blue With one gray glimpse of sea.' No doubt he would have been delighted with the Portsmouth electrics which, apart from a few flashes on frosty nights, did nothing, unlike steam trains, to obscure the view. *Box collection, National Railway Museum, York*

The dining saloon of a 4RES unit. Twenty-nine 4CORs were built originally, plus 18 4RESs. The former consisted of two 3rd Class motor brake saloons with 52 seats, a 68-seat corridor 3rd, and a 54-seat corridor composite; the latter had similar motor brake saloons, whilst the trailer vehicles were a 3rd Class restaurant and kitchen car and a composite with a dining saloon. It has been claimed that the reduced power of the Portsmouth units was a regressive move, but a total horsepower for a 12-coach unit of 3,300 was more than adequate, and Sir Herbert Walker, the Southern Railway General Manager, had always made it clear that electrification was intended to bring greater reliability and frequency rather than dramatically higher speeds. *National Railway Museum, York*

Although they looked thoroughly up-to-date with their sheet steel-panelled sides and flush-fitting windows, the 4CORs, like all pre-war Southern Electrics, were constructed in a traditional manner, as this picture of the complex wooden framing lurking beneath a trailer car of the preserved unit No 3142 clearly shows.

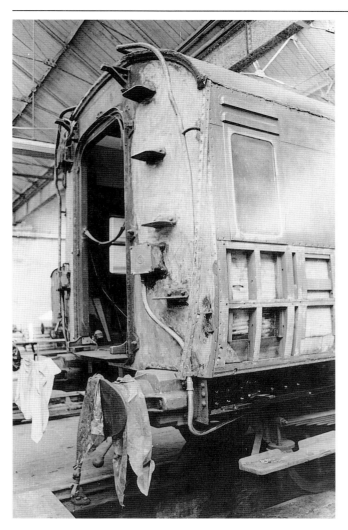

No shortage of varnished wood in the 3rd Class compartment of this 4COR trailer car! *National Railway Museum, York*

A year later, in July 1938, the former LB&SCR Mid-Sussex line from Three Bridges, and from Mitcham Junction and Dorking, through Horsham and Arundel to Bognor Regis and Portsmouth joined the electrified empire.

The Chairman of Bognor Regis Council, Mr T. W. Marshall, after travelling on the inaugural electric train, remarked:

> There must be many of us who from our boyhood have been fascinated by the steam engine and who will regret its passing, especially since from its early days the Brighton line has been noted for the excellence of its locomotive design, but as the Latin poet says

'Times change and we must change with them', and those who may draw a sigh at the passing of the steam locomotive will, I am sure, quickly take to their hearts the slick modernity of the new electric trains.

Presumably he couldn't lay hands on a Latin poet's views on the 'B4X' 4-4-0s which hauled many of the Mid-Sussex line expresses.

A week later the *West Sussex Observer* recorded that 'A horse which strayed from an adjoining field was killed by an electric shock on the Southern Railway near Lewisham Junction yesterday. The services were interrupted for an hour.'

Twenty-six more 4CORs and 13 4BUF buffet units were built for the new service, the latter of a distinctly art deco design, the handiwork of the new CME, Oliver Bulleid; 68 more 2BILs were also built. 4BUF No 3085 is seen here before entering service. The lighter shade of green applied to the buffet car is immediately apparent. *National Railway Museum, York*

The remarkable interior of a 4BUF buffet car. Amongst the many curious ideas that Oliver Bulleid inflicted on the travelling public was the one that it didn't wish to see where it was going whilst eating or drinking. He was to do it again with the notorious steam-hauled 'tavern cars' after the war. As a piece of avant garde design the 4BUF buffet cars were worthy of an award. Just so long as you didn't wish to partake of refreshments in one. *National Railway Museum, York*

The 9.33 am Victoria to Bognor Regis, headed by 2BIL No 2068, passes former LB&SCR 'C2X' Class 0-6-0 No 32534 with a Horsham-bound goods train near Christs Hospital. It has to be remembered that throughout the Southern Railway's extensive electrification programme goods traffic remained almost the exclusive preserve of steam. *John Scrace*

The last batch of 2BILs was built for the Reading line electrification in the autumn of 1938. A train from Waterloo, with unit No 2016 leading, arrives at Reading General in the spring of 1969, long after the former South Eastern & Chatham station at Reading had been closed and Southern services diverted up the bank to new platforms constructed at the former GWR station. The Southern electrified Waterloo route could not rival the steam-operated GWR one to Paddington for speed, but was chiefly of value for the busy intermediate stations of Wokingham, Bracknell, Ascot, Virginia Water, Staines and Richmond - hence the provision of semi-fast rather than express units.

No 2147 at Ascot on 29 November 1938. *National Railway Museum, York*

The last long-distance electrification scheme before the outbreak of war was that to the Medway; the full electric service from Charing Cross, Cannon Street and Victoria to Maidstone, Rochester, Chatham and Gillingham was inaugurated in July 1939. It was not a very long distance and, as with the Reading scheme, semi-fast units were deemed suitable, and 76 two-car units were built.

Successors to the 2BILs, these were the 2HALs, which, believe it or not, meant 'half a lavatory'! A backward step in just about every way from their predecessors, the half lavatory wasn't to be taken literally; what it meant was that only half the passengers in each unit had access to the lavatory. This was because only the driving trailer composites had corridors, the motor coaches containing seven 3rd Class compartments.

The HALs were designed by Bulleid and were a

foretaste of his notion of packing in as many passengers as possible regardless of comfort, which reached its full and ghastly fruition in his first suburban units two years later.

Wooden framed and steel panelled, the HALs had welded steel front ends which, whilst similar to the BILs, were more angular and less attractive. They had mean little windows and hard, narrow, uncomfortable bench-type seats, while the dignified varnished wooden panelling of the Maunsell units was replaced by grey paint which looked like undercoat waiting to be decently covered up. I write from bitter experience, for there was a period when I was serving Her Majesty as a typist at RAF West Malling and I regularly travelled in the HALs. I didn't much like returning to camp anyway, and a 40-minute ride in a HAL was a suitably depressing prelude.

A 3rd Class compartment of a 2HAL. *National Railway Museum, York*

A rake of four 2HALs passes Bromley on a trial run on 24 May 1939. *H. C. Casserley*

A Maidstone West to Victoria service of four 2HALs, headed by No 2657, approaches Bickley on 27 July 1966. *Brian Morrison*

Not all Maidstone services were operated by long-distance stock. Here is 4SUB No 4486 on a Cannon Street to Maidstone East train *circa* 1945. *National Railway Museum, York*

I got my own back on 12 months of miserable HAL travel on the evening of 15 January 1958. This was the day I was demobbed and I celebrated by catching the one steam train of the day which stopped at West Malling; it came up from the coast and terminated at Holborn Viaduct. I luxuriated in the relative comfort of a BR Mark 1 corridor as we steamed through the night safe in the charge of an elderly but reliable 4-4-0. The train returned to the Kent coast next morning as the 7.24 am London Bridge (although it actually started from Holborn Viaduct) to Deal, and is seen here leaving Tonbridge in the charge of 'D1' No 31739 on 3 June 1961, ten days before the second phase of the Kent coast electrification removed all steam workings.

One of the great advantages of electrification was its cleanliness, as indeed it still is in this era of concern for the environment. Multiple unit carriages were inherently cleaner than steam-locomotive-hauled ones and, to ensure that they stayed that way, washing plants were set up throughout the system. Here 3SUB No 1401 is seen being scrubbed at Norwood on 5 May 1938. *Author's collection*

The war brought to an end any expansion of the electrified network for the duration, but 16 2HALs, Nos 2677-92, were under construction to augment the Reading services, which had become very popular with electrification. Early in 1940 two additional 4LAV units entered service. Although of the same layout as their predecessors these two units, Nos 2954/5, were in other respects identical to the 2HALs as this official picture of No 2956 clearly shows. *National Railway Museum, York*

Much of the Battle of Britain in the late summer of 1940 and the Blitz which it inaugurated was fought over Southern Electric territory. The county borough of Croydon suffered particularly and Selhurst depot received a direct hit. LSWR-built 3SUB No 1259 was one of the minor casualties. *National Railway Museum, York*

Portsmouth Harbour station on the morning of 13 August 1940. A helmeted fireman is damping down the smouldering remains of 2BIL No 2102 destroyed when the station was bombed. The station was not re-opened until after the war, but although this is said to have been because of the extensive damage, one wonders if the reasons were actually strategic; the track on the far right was clearly sufficiently serviceable for a steam locomotive to shunt in a rake of open wagons to take away the debris. *National Railway Museum, York*

A scene outside 'Waterloo Main Line' on 6 September 1940 after an air raid, with two tracks, complete with third rail, suspended over a crater. This was the beginning of a period, lasting until May of the following year, when the 2¼ miles between Queens Road, Battersea, and Waterloo would be bombed 92 times, making it the most heavily attacked section of railway line in the country. *National Railway Museum, York*

Clearing up at Eastbourne station on 4 May 1942 after an air raid. *National Railway Museum, York*

Troops embarking at Newhaven, 11 June 1944, D-Day plus 5. *National Railway Museum, York*

A poignant picture of American GIs at Waterloo waiting to board a train for Portsmouth at the time of D-Day. *National Railway Museum, York*

It had always been the Southern Railway's long-term objective to abandon steam entirely, and towards this end the design of two 1,470 hp Co-Co electric locomotives was well advanced in September 1939. Work continued, and the first, No CC1, entered service in 1941, the second, CC2, two years later. The two locomotives proved themselves well able to haul the heaviest goods trains and regularly worked over the mid-Sussex line. When peace resumed they also found employment on the Newhaven boat trains. In order to get over the problem of gaps in the third rail, a motor generator set was provided fitted with a flywheel. The locomotives were also equipped with pantographs so that they could take current from overhead wires in goods yards where it would have been too dangerous to lay the third rail, but in the event they were almost never used. No CC2 is pictured here when new at Bognor. *Author's collection*

5 Post-war developments: 1945-59

Full employment, a Labour government, an all-round increase in living standards but continuing restrictions on private motoring meant that Southern Electrics were busier than ever in the late 1940s carrying day-trippers and holidaymakers to the countryside and the sea.

When my form master organised a visit from our school at Croydon to an air display at Gatwick in June 1949 I looked forward eagerly to my first ride down the Brighton line in a main-line electric, a 6PUL or a 6PAN, or a 4LAV at least. Bitter was my disappointment when a pre-Grouping 4SUB pulled into the platform at East Croydon. In fact, suburban units were regularly seen beyond the suburban area for special events, at Bank Holidays and on summer weekends. They could develop a fair turn of speed, but their harsh riding, fairly cramped accommodation and absence of lavatories did not endear them to patrons.

A unit converted from former SECR steam stock on a Victoria-Coulsdon North service entering East Croydon in April 1950. *Author's collection*

The first main-line EMUs to be built after the war were seven 2HALs, Nos 2693-9. Although of similar layout to their pre-war predecessors, they looked just like contemporary all-steel suburban units with their flat fronts, rounded body profile and toplights above the doors. Internally they were a good deal better than the pre-war HALs. Here No 2698 leads a pre-war 2HAL along the Ouse Valley on a Brighton to Seaford working (despite the headcode which should have taken the pair no further than Lewes) in the summer of 1968.

Pullmans were withdrawn during the war but the 'Brighton Belle' reappeared in all its former glory in 1947 and resumed where it had left off. Unit No 3053 rattles through Three Bridges with the 3 pm Victoria to Brighton on 1 September 1964. *John Scrace*

Similarly the Pullmans were restored to the 6PUL units. Here we see a 6PUL bringing up the rear of the 11.45 am Victoria to Ore headed by a 6PAN passing South Croydon on 17 May 1964. *John Scrace*

All-steel Bulleid 4SUBs were steadily replacing the old wooden-bodied stock and, like their predecessors, sometimes escaped far beyond the London suburbs, as No 4706 hurrying through Berwick on the Eastbourne-Lewes line in 1969.

The Waterloo to Windsor and Weybridge lines had been electrified in 1936 and a final batch of 2NOLs had been produced to work these and the Reading route. Being of a semi-fast nature, these services demanded 1st Class accommodation, but after the war this was abolished. 2NOL No 1851 from Reading and Windsor arrives at Waterloo ahead of LMS-built 'Duchess' Class 'Pacific' No 46236 *City of Bradford* with the 'Atlantic Coast Express' on 22 June 1948; the Stanier 'Pacific' was taking part in the locomotive exchanges of that year. *C. C. B. Herbert, National Railway Museum, York*

Steam continued to monopolise the Kent coast beyond the Medway towns and with the resumption of travel to the Continent demand soon returned to, then outstripped, pre-war levels. The new Bulleid 'Pacifics' had charge of much of the boat train traffic, and here the pioneer, the appropriately named *Channel Packet*, is about to leave Dover Marine for Victoria. *J. G. Click*

However, there was one boat train which, from May 1949, was handed over to electric haulage, to the three Bulleid/Raworth locomotives, although reliefs were still steam powered. This was the Newhaven service, which is seen here passing Tooting Bec behind No 20002 (the former CC2 - see page 38) on 17 September 1966. Nos 20001-3 virtually monopolised the Newhaven boat train from 1949 until their withdrawal in the spring of 1969.

The Victoria-Newhaven-Dieppe-Paris service, being slightly cheaper than its rivals, was popular with students and the backpack fraternity. One of my fellow student porters at Victoria once stood rather too close to the Newhaven boat train as it pulled out on a summer afternoon in 1960 and had his cap removed by a young Frenchman, a typical example of sophisticated Gallic wit. *Charles Whetmath*

A third electric locomotive, No 20003, was introduced in 1949. It was similar to its two predecessors but could instantly be spotted by its flat front ends. All three worked freight, particularly on the Mid-Sussex line, with considerable success, but as we have just seen they also appeared on various passenger duties.

Holiday traffic of all descriptions boomed in the 1950s and, although car ownership was shooting up, the majority still travelled either by motor coach or rail. Through trains from other regions to the Sussex coast were big business in the summer time, and while there was little scope for electric haulage as yet, the three electric locomotives sometimes took over from foreign steam at Clapham Junction. No 20003 is about to set off from Brighton with a returning Western Region train in the summer of 1960. *Author's collection*

Nevertheless one was much more likely to make the entire journey by steam. 'N' Class 2-6-0 No 31875, in third rail territory, passes Epsom on 26 July 1959 with a train of GWR-built carriages heading for Bognor Regis. *R. H. Tunstall*

Shortly before 7.30 am on the morning of 25 August 1958 the Glasgow to Eastbourne car sleeper, hauled by a BR Standard Class '5MT' 4-6-0, was signalled on to the wrong track on the approach to Eastbourne station and ran into the 6.50 am Hastings to London Bridge express; the latter, a 12-coach train, was stationary. A signal gantry was brought down, the massive motor car of the leading 6PUL unit was thrown on to its side and badly knocked about, whilst the corridor 2nd immediately behind was telescoped into it. Five passengers were killed and 25 injured, almost all off of them in these two vehicles. As can be seen, the steam engine remained upright and the LMS-built carriages of its train were virtually undamaged. *National Railway Museum, York*

Steam would not survive much longer. The 1955 Modernisation Plan spelled out its demise and the next stage of the Southern's grand scheme to expel steam entirely was announced - this was the Kent coast electrification.

In 1956 the first of the eagerly awaited BR Standard express EMUs were completed. Similar in many respects to current BR Mark 1 steam stock with wood-panelled interiors, their layout was based on that of their predecessors, the pre-war Southern Railway 4CORs. There were four 4CEPB units, Nos 7101-4, composed of two motor brake driving saloons with a corridor 2nd and a corridor composite between them. There were also two 4BEPB units, Nos 7001/2, in which the corridor second was replaced by a buffet car.

The last Saturday of steam at Ramsgate, 13 June 1959. 'Schools' Class 4-4-0 No 30919 *Harrow leaves* with an express from Victoria whilst in the background 4CEPs and 4BEPs wait to take over on the Monday morning.

Above 4CEPB No 7104 stands in Brighton station on 26 January 1979. On rebuilding unit 7104 became 1502.

Right One of the prototype 4CEPs (the B was soon dropped) can be seen in the distance in the sidings at Reigate in 1971. Prominent are semaphore signals, still to be found on many parts of the Southern electric at this time.

Below The CEPs took over many of the boat train duties from steam. A train from Victoria headed by No 1553, as later renumbered, stands amongst the plethora of handsome Victoria ironwork of Dover Marine (Western Docks as it had by then become) in the summer of 1985.

The first of the production 4CEPs, No 7105, seen on completion in September 1958. Compared to the prototypes they had unpainted sliding vents, which brightened up their uninspiring appearance and livery just a little. At this time all EMUs were still painted in the traditional not very bright green. Without lining, spots, stripes or stars, or smoke or steam coming out of the front, they could look pretty sombre. *Colin Marsden collection*

The prototypes had wood veneer panelling, the production units, as seen in this picture, rather more cheerful plastics. *Colin Marsden collection*

To work slow and semi-fast Kent coast services several series of two-car units, the 2HAPs, were built. Their designation makes clear that they were intended as successors for the 2HALs; as with the HALs, only one coach of a 2HAP had access to a lavatory. The bodies of the earliest units were of Southern Railway design, more or less identical to the suburban 4EPBs, a remarkable situation in view of the fact that the Southern Railway had been dead for the best part of ten years, but perhaps on reflection not really so remarkable given the Southern Electric's predilection for taking two steps forward and one step back. Later 2HAPs were of BR standard design.

The HAPs have undergone various modifications over the years, and have worked all over the Southern network, although they have not lasted particularly well and most have been taken out of service. Here we see a coincidence of HAPs, Nos 4308 (originally 6077) and 4309 (originally 6078) at Clapham Junction on 29 August 1991.

Close relations of the HAPs are the 2EPBs. These were designed as suburban two-coach units without lavatories, of semi-saloon layout. Nevertheless they have often found themselves working slow and semi-fast services well beyond the London suburbs. Again their bodies are of both Southern Railway and British Railways design. One of the earlier SR-type units, No 6329, facelifted with the interior partitions removed, stands alongside a 4CIG under the great arch of Brighton station on a November evening in 1988 before setting off for Eastbourne and Hastings. Not the least remarkable thing about the HAPs and EPBs is that some of them were built on underframes from withdrawn 2NOLs - in other words a fair part of them dates back to the 1930s. The Southern Electric is a most frugal concern which has always got its money's worth out of everything it owns.

BR-type 2EPB No 6412 leaves Snodland with the 14.21 Strood to Paddock Wood on 10 May 1986. *Chris Wilson*

6 The 1960s - old and new: 1960-66

Unlike all other Southern electrification schemes, the Kent Coast one was designed to sweep steam away entirely. To this end 24 electric locomotives were built at Doncaster in 1959-60, capable of hauling all goods traffic and any passenger trains, such as the 'Golden Arrow' and the 'Night Ferry', not suitable for EMUs. A development of the three Southern Co-Co locomotives, the 24 were of similar power but lighter Bo-Bos of 2,552 hp; they were fitted with four English Electric spring-borne traction motors. Numbered E5000-23, a good deal of thought had gone into their appearance, Mischa Black of the Design Research Unit being responsible for their styling. He also worked on the early West Coast electric locomotives, the 'Warships' and the 'Westerns', and as a consequence Nos E5000-23 were rather sleek-looking with pale grey cab window surrounds and a red and grey stripe along their sides.

The now preserved No E5001 at Waterloo.

The best known duty of the E5000s, or Class '71s' as they later became, was the haulage of the 'Golden Arrow'. By the early 1960s the prestige of this all-Pullman express was beginning to decline, air travel between London and Paris being much faster. Ordinary 2nd Class carriages replaced many of the Pullmans, but the locomotive still proudly carried the 'Golden Arrow' headboard and the French and British flags. Here we see a scene in the late 1960s just before departure from the traditional platform 8 - a 4SUB stands in the adjoining, Central Section, platform 9.

The 'Golden Arrow' ceased to run in 1972, although its connecting French counterpart, the 'Flèche D'Or', continued for a little while longer. Three or four Pullmans sufficed at the end and these lost their names, were repainted into British Rail corporate blue and grey with thick white lining and over-large unshaded 'Golden Arrow' insignia, a far cry from their former glories. In its final year a porter carries luggage into S302S, the former 'Phoenix', one of the ten cars built in 1951/2.

Was ever a carriage better named? The wheel has now turned full circle, for 'Phoenix' was bought by John Sherwood and restored to work the Victoria to Folkestone section of the Venice-Simplon-Orient Express. More magnificent than ever, with the post-war square toilet window replaced by the traditional oval one, the restored 'Phoenix' is seen at platform 2, Victoria station, 19 years on from the previous picture, on 29 August 1991, about to depart for Folkestone Harbour. Next to 'Phoenix' is the former 'Brighton Belle' car, 'Vera'.

The last of the pre-war suburban EMUs, of LB&SCR origin, which still worked down to the coast on occasions until the end of their days, was withdrawn in 1962. Unit No 1600, in its original 3SUB form, is seen here at New Beckenham in November 1946. *Colin Marsden collection*

The second stage of the Kent Coast electrification, through Tonbridge and Ashford to the coast, in June 1961 saw the end of scenes such as this. 'Schools' Class 4-4-0 No 30924 *Haileybury* accelerates through Bickley with a Victoria to Ramsgate express.

The Kent coast electrification saw the removal of the 2HALs from the Medway services and their transfer to the Central Section. Up and down HALs meet on the Lewes to Seaford line beneath the South Downs in the winter of 1969.

The Class '71' electric locomotives had not proved a total success and were little used on freight work chiefly because, although there were one or two yards such as Hither Green which were fitted with overhead electrification, if there was no third rail, it was no go. Ten '71s' were converted to Class '74' electro-diesels but they proved troublesome and unreliable and all were withdrawn by the early 1980s. No E5014 stands at New Cross with vans for North Kent in September 1969.

The Class '73' electro-diesels were more successful. These, in addition to their four 400 hp traction motors, were fitted with a 600 hp English Electric diesel engine. This meant that they could work, admittedly at reduced power, over non-electrified tracks. Six, Nos E6001-6, were built in 1962 and a further 45 in 1967 for the Bournemouth electrification. One of the first batch, in charge of a van train from Bricklayers Arms to Coulsdon North (both destinations now vanished), is overtaken by a clerestory-roofed London Underground train at New Cross Gate in May 1969.

Because of their limited power off the third rail, the '73s' were very rarely seen hauling passenger trains for any distance when working as diesels. However, in emergencies this could happen. On the morning of 16 June 1984 two were sent out by Bournemouth depot as substitutes for a failed Class '33' diesel locomotive to collect the 06.45 Channel Islands boat train from Weymouth Quay. They are seen here passing Wareham, having worked up a fair turn of speed on the long straight stretch through Wool.

The three original Southern electric locomotives continued to soldier on through the 1960s. No 20002, repainted in Brunswick green livery, has charge of the Royal Train carrying the Queen and the Duke of Edinburgh to the 1965 Derby as it passes a 4EPB suburban unit at East Croydon on its way to Tattenham Corner. Previously this duty had been allocated to a 'Schools' Class 4-4-0. *Duncan Simmonds*

As steam faded away, through services from other Regions were put in charge of diesel locomotives. No D5067, a Derby/Sulzer Class Bo-Bo (later Class '24)', approaches Honor Oak Park with a rake of Eastern Region non-corridor carriages, some of LNER origin, forming the 9.10 am Hitchin-Brighton on 3 June 1962. *John Scrace*

Most passenger services on non-electrified lines were taken over by diesel-electric multiple units. These had much in common with EMUs and, indeed, it was stated at the time of their building that the DEMUs could be converted to EMUS should their routes be electrified. At Redhill in the mid-1970s a 1957 3H unit (left) sets off for Tonbridge, whilst standing on the site of the former shed, to the right of the Class '73' electro-diesel, is a 1962 3D unit, built for the Oxted line.

But steam was not quite gone. The snow and ice of January 1966 taxed the heating capabilities of diesel locomotives and as a consequence Bulleid 'light Pacifics' reappeared on the Brighton to Plymouth train. Smoke and steam envelope a couple of 2BILs as the train departs westwards on a bitterly cold early January morning.

The very last steam run down the Brighton main line took place on 19 March 1967 when rebuilt Bulleid 'Pacific' No 34108 *Wincanton* had charge of a special. It is seen here approaching Balcombe Tunnel. *John Scrace*

January 1963 marked the 30th anniversary of the Brighton line electrification, but the event passed largely unnoticed - which would surely not be the case today.

Elsewhere on British Rail change was everything. BR-designed carriages were swiftly replacing the few remaining pre-Nationalisation ones, and steam was in terminal decline, largely giving way to diesel and electric multiple units and locomotives. Dr Beeching was in charge and, with the enthusiastic backing of a Conservative government, modernisation went hand in hand with sweeping branch-line and some main-line closures.

The Central Section of the Southern was virtually untouched by this revolution, seemingly existing in a time warp, its services operated by the same green electric multiple units which had been there since the 1930s.

There was just branch line on the Southern Electric that closed in this period, that from Haywards Heath to Horsted Keynes, in 1963. Although in theory part of a through route from London to the coast, it had seldom been used as such, particularly as there was no third rail north of Horsted Keynes; an hourly service of stopping trains, worked by NOLs and BILs, had run between there and Seaford.

A somewhat sleepy branch, it sprang to eminence at the eleventh hour - in its final two years - when in April 1961 the Bluebell Railway commenced running its preserved steam trains between Sheffield Park and Horsted Keynes.

The branch was latterly run as single track, the down line being used to store condemned coaching stock, which for a time stretched all of 2 miles and from which source the Bluebell drew its first carriages.

A 32-year-old 6PUL, No 3015, brings up the rear of a Victoria to Eastbourne, Hastings and Ore express as it snakes out of Lewes on a summer's day in 1965. *Charles Whetmath*

Elderly 4LAV No 2947 pulls out of Hassocks on a Victoria to Brighton stopping train in August 1967.

A ten-coach train made up of 2HAL and 2BILs leaves Redhill for Brighton in June 1969.

The 4CIGs, originally numbered 7301-7438 and the 29 BIGs, buffet units numbered 7031-58, achieved the interesting (although not in Southern terms unique) feat of being both revolutionary and antiquated at the same time. Introduced in 1964, they rode considerably better than their predecessors - I was agreeably impressed by this on first acquaintance - in comparison with the lurching, thumping progress of the motor coaches of the PULs and PANs. But they were of Mark 1 profile and design which was by now obsolete elsewhere on British Rail. Built at York, there was no doubting their 4COR ancestry by way of the 4CEPs. They were given slightly more shapely fibreglass cab fronts but I'm not sure that this made them any better looking.

Changing travelling habits meant that the two luggage vans provided in each of the earlier units were no longer needed, so a single guard's/luggage van was provided in the middle non-driving motor 2nd saloon. There were two driving composites and a trailer 2nd saloon. Bright yellow warning panels had been found necessary elsewhere on BR diesels and electrics (noisy, smoky steam locomotives were a lot easier for permanent way gangs to spot) and these were now applied to Southern electrics. The livery was still green, but not for much longer.

In reality time was running out for the first-generation Southern electrics. First to be replaced were the venerable 6PULs and PANs, their successors being the 4CIGs and 4BIGs.

4CIG No 7334 heads a Victoria-Ore express through Pevensey Bay Halt at approximately the spot where William of Normandy landed on his way to meet Harold of Wessex and become the Conqueror (the greaseproof paper his mother had wrapped his sandwiches in is blowing about on the platform behind the train). Ore, by the way, is an insignificant station on the outskirts of Hastings; it just happens that for operational reasons it has always been convenient to terminate electric services there.

4CIG No 7302 arrives at Hastings from Victoria in October 1969.

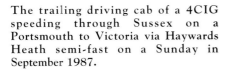

The trailing driving cab of a 4CIG speeding through Sussex on a Portsmouth to Victoria via Haywards Heath semi-fast on a Sunday in September 1987.

Very quickly the small yellow panel grew to cover the entire front of multiple units as seen here on 4COR No 3113 travelling at speed south of Haywards Heath with a London Bridge-Littlehampton rush-hour express in July 1967. By this date the 4CORs were being fitted with roller-blind number indicators in place of stencils, it being considered that they, unlike all other Southern Railway-built EMUs, were not yet time-expired.

A further change in livery, equally startling, was introduced in 1964. Green, which I had always assumed could only be changed on Southern Electrics by Act of Parliament, began to give way to blue, and the 'double arrow' would become the universal BR symbol. A 4COR arrives at Eastbourne on a Brighton-Ore stopping service on a summer Saturday in 1969 so attired.

For a few years all sorts of variations of liveries were to be found on the Southern. In the sidings is a train of locomotive-hauled stock from the Eastern Region, most of it still in maroon, the brake 2nd bearing the BR badge applied to carriages. Behind it is a 4CIG in green, and beside that a 4BIG in blue and grey.

Blue and grey was the livery chosen for Inter-City stock, but for some obscure reason this was initially deemed inappropriate for Southern express multiple units and they were repainted in all-over blue, which was as dull as the previous dark green. However, sense soon prevailed. A Victoria to Ramsgate express passes Sevenoaks in March 1969 - the leading 4CEP, No 7182, and the 4BEP unit are still in green, but the trailing 4CEP is in the new blue and grey livery.

The pioneer 4CIG, No 7301, speeds through the woods south of Haywards Heath with a Victoria to Littlehampton express in August 1967, still in green but with all-yellow ends; next is a blue and grey 4BIG, whilst a green 4CIG brings up the rear. None of the 4CIGs or 4BIGs ever wore all-over blue.

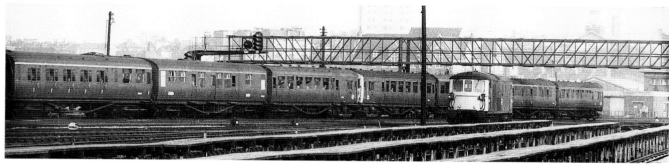

Top left No 4LAV ever acquired blue livery and only two received all-yellow ends but many, although certainly not all, of the 4CORs, 4BUFs, 4GRIs, 2BILs and 2HALs went blue and yellow at their final repaint. 2BIL No 2098 stands at platform 8 at Lewes, having just arrived on the short journey from Seaford, in April 1969. It still carries the headcode 'I', although the rear lamp has been attached ready for the return journey. It was extraordinary that throughout their careers the Southern Railway EMUs were always equipped with rear oil-lamps.

Centre left A curious rebuilding as late as 1962 was that of the restaurant cars from three 4RESs. The Southern still couldn't bring itself to use the term 'buffet' so officially they were called 'griddles', hence the designation 4GRI; even more curiously they bore both 'griddle' and 'buffet' on their bodysides. These bodysides were completely new and the combination of BR-type windows and a pre-war Southern profile showed how handsome BR Mark 1s might have been had they not perpetuated Bulleid's idiosyncratic curved outline. One of the griddle cars is the sixth vehicle in this London Bridge-Eastbourne express passing a Class '73' in the sidings at New Cross Gate in May 1970.

Bottom left All sorts of curious things happened to the 4COR family in its final years. The 4RES units were reformed at the beginning of 1964, and two such examples are seen here passing Tooting Bec, between Balham and Streatham, on a Victoria to Littlehampton express during that summer. No 3067 has a former 6PUL trailer 2nd in place of its kitchen 2nd, whilst the middle unit has a former 6PUL Pullman. *Charles Whetmath*

Above Meanwhile, on the Portsmouth direct line little had changed. An up express consisting of two 4CORs flanking a 4BUF passes Whitton Junction, having been diverted via Chertsey, on 28 November 1965. *Charles Whetmath*

Below Another 12-coach train, headed by 4COR No 3102, this time a down express diverted via the New Line and seen near Hampton Court Junction in March 1965. *Charles Whetmath*

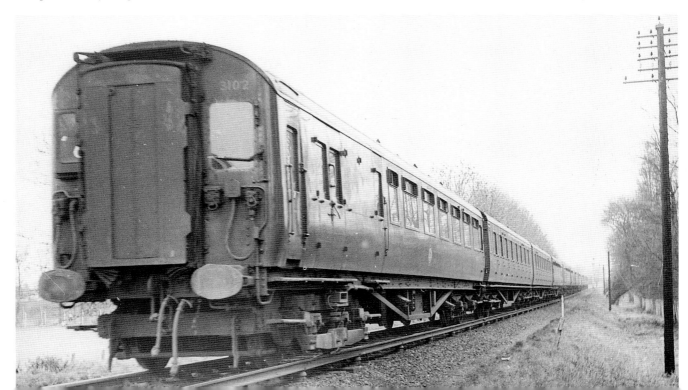

7 On to Bournemouth: 1967-72

Electrification came to the Bournemouth line on 10 July 1967. Officially that is. For several weeks before, in true Southern tradition, electric trains had been operating some services, but from that date onwards steam was no more.

Electrification to Southampton and Bournemouth had been on the cards for many years before the announcement was made in September 1964; it was very much in the Southern tradition established with the Brighton scheme more than 30 years earlier, multiple units operating both express and stopping services.

Few of the vehicles which made up the express units were in fact new. Investment for the new electric service being severely limited, of the 160 carriages only the 22 motor 2nds of the 4REPs were new, the rest being converted steam stock, an echo of Southern Railway suburban practice of the 1920s and '30s. The Bournemouth units were almost identical in appearance to the Brighton line CIGs and BIGs.

There was insufficient money to extend the third rail to Poole, Wareham and Weymouth. A push-pull fitted Class '33' diesel-electric locomotive would therefore couple on to the one or two 4TC units at Bournemouth, the 4REP would uncouple, ready to work back to Waterloo, and the '33' would have charge for the rest of the journey.

Motor coach (MSO) No S62148, of one of the Waterloo-Bournemouth 4REP express units, No 3004, is seen at York Works on 23 July 1967 shortly before entering service. Each of the 11 REPs produced no less than 3,200 hp, but this was needed to propel not only itself but up to a further eight carriages, 12 being the standard formation between Waterloo and Bournemouth. *Colin Marsden collection*

4REP No 3009, hauling two 4TCs, arriving at Basingstoke at the head of a 12-coach Bournemouth to Waterloo semi-fast in January 1986. In addition to the original 11 4REPs, Nos 3001-11, each of which consisted of two motor 2nd saloons flanking a corridor trailer brake 1st and buffet car, there were 29 4TC non-powered units, Nos 401-28, each consisting of a trailer corridor 1st, trailer corridor brake 2nd and two driving trailer open 2nds.

A Waterloo train, consisting of a Class '33' and a 4TC, south of Dorchester on a snowy February day in 1973.

To work the stopping services a new type of four-car unit was produced. This was the 4VEP. All the Bournemouth units, both express and main line, were originally painted blue, despite the fact that on all other regions of British Rail blue and white was the standard InterCity livery. Not only this, but the outmoded Mark 1 outline was used, where elsewhere the Mark 2 had been in production for some years.

Someone once described the 4VEPs as 4SUBs with corridors. Seating was arranged in threes and twos in the 2nd Class on thin cushions, and there were but two lavatories for the 48 1st Class and 232 2nd Class passengers that each 4VEP could accommodate.

All things considered, the Bournemouth electrification scheme was a pretty cut-price second-rate affair. One great advantage of the BR-designed express units was that, unlike the old PULs, PANs, CORs, etc, they could work with semi-fast and suburban units. At least it was a great advantage for the operating authorities, but not quite so wonderful for the customers who, ever since their introduction, have often had to put up with the limited splendours of a 4VEP on a long-distance run when they have had every right to expect something better.

4VEPs under construction at Derby Works in 1966. *Colin Marsden collection*

No 7710, temporarily transferred to the Central Section, is seen at Gatwick Airport early in its career in September 1969.

Two VEPs seen after the Weymouth line was eventually electrified. No 3072 (originally 7772) is nearest the camera in the sidings at Weymouth, whilst a Class '33' propels two 4TCs up the bank past the site of Radipole Halt in November 1988.

The conversion of the branch from Brockenhurst to Lymington was part of the Bournemouth electrification scheme. In the steam era boat trains had been worked directly to Waterloo, hauled in early BR days by Drummond 4-4-0s, later by Maunsell 'Schools'. Nowadays 4VEPs generally work the branch, connecting with expresses at Brockenhurst. Here a train approaches Lymington Quay in August 1991.

Left Internally, as this view of a 4REP buffet car shows, the carriages of the express units were bright and cheerful and quite comfortable, although the riding qualities of the buffet cars in particular deteriorated rapidly after some while out of works, until they were quite as bad as the original Brighton line 6PUL and 6PAN motor cars; any patrons attempting to drink hot tea or coffee, particularly through the curving New Forest section, stood an excellent chance of scalding themselves.

Below left Nevertheless, electrification brought more business and in the early days electro-diesels regularly augmented the 4REPs. A Class '73' has charge of two 4TCs passing Clapham Junction with a Waterloo to Bournemouth express in February 1968. Eventually four more 4REPs, Nos 3012-5, and three 4TCs, Nos 432-4, were built in 1974, whilst in the same year three 3TCs, nos 429-31, were converted to standard four-coach units.

The Isle of Wight has always been quite different from the rest of the Southern network, if only because its rolling-stock has consisted of living museum pieces. When the decision was taken to electrify the surviving Ryde-Shanklin section, the tunnel at Ryde dictated that normal-size carriages could not be used. The shoestring budget ruled out any possibility of new stock, so BR bought some time-expired London Transport tube trains. They were better than nothing and ensured that the railways kept their tenuous foothold on the island, but as one would expect of vehicles built for commuter work in the 1920s and early '30s, they were cramped and very rough riding.

Five-car unit No 485 044 passes diesel shunter No 03079 on the outskirts of Ryde on 9 August 1986. *David Brown*

Left The first 20 4VEPs were built for the Bournemouth line and these were immediately followed by 35 more units which replaced the faithful 35-year-old 4LAVs on the Brighton line. A 4VEP from Brighton arrives at East Croydon during a snowstorm in February 1969.

Below 1969 saw the end of the 4LAVs, the very first main-line EMUs built by the Southern Railway back in 1932. No 2925 at the head of a London Bridge to Reigate and Brighton stopping train passes South Croydon on one of its last runs.

Below Although the Brighton line 6PULs and 6PANs had been withdrawn before the 4LAVs, some were reformed into 6CORs and worked relief services for a short while, even appearing on the South Eastern Section. They too were withdrawn in late 1968 and early 1969. One unit stands at Gatwick Airport, flanked by 2BILs, in the summer of 1969.

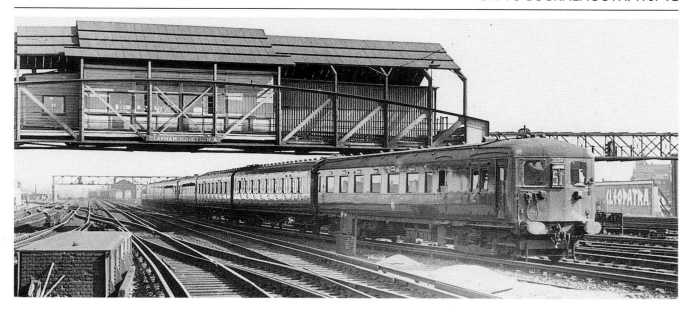

Above In the summer of 1965 the motor coaches from 6PULs Nos 3017/8 were used to replace damaged motor coaches of 4CORs Nos 3124/48. Permanently coupled to form an eight-car unit with the former PUL motor coaches at each end, one of their regular workings was the 19.17 Waterloo-Farnham, seen here passing under Clapham Junction 'A' box. *Charles Whetmath*

Right Just one 6COR, No 3045, was repainted in blue livery with all-yellow ends and was fitted with BR-style horns instead of the usual whistle. It is seen at Selhurst depot in November 1968.

Below right Even so, this was not quite the end. A Mobile Laboratory Unit S15 was formed of two 6PAN motor coaches, Nos 11057/8, and Pullmans 'Ruth' and 'Bertha' from 6PUL units, seen here at Coulsdon North sidings in October 1968. In fact, the unit was never used as such and the two motor coaches were eventually broken up in South Wales in 1971. The Pullmans, however, survived, 'Ruth' being preserved by the 6000 Locomotive Association at Hereford, whilst 'Bertha' is still at work in Sussex, on the Bluebell Railway.

Far right There is also a trailer composite surviving from a PUL/PAN unit, which, as can be seen in this view looking along its corridor, will need a vast amount of work done on it before it is fit for passenger service. After languishing in various parts of the country it has found a home at Swanage.

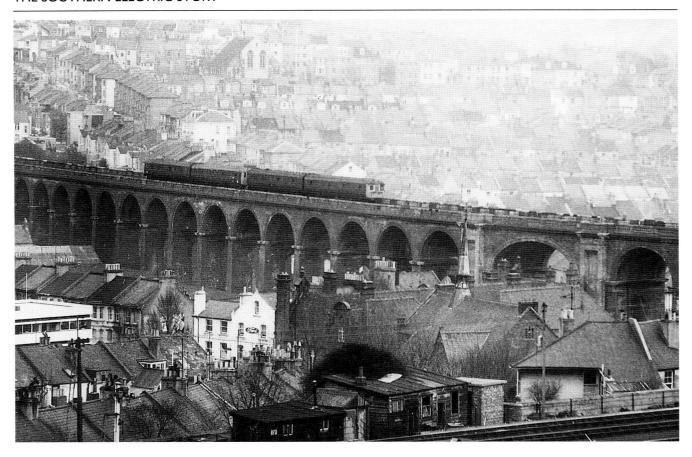

With the 4LAVs all gone, the Southern set about replacing the 2BILs with more 4VEPs. A pair of 2BILs, one in Southern green, the other in BR blue livery, is seen crossing the famous London Road Viaduct at Brighton in the winter of 1970/71 shortly before withdrawal.

Although the 6PULs and PANs were gone, their famous contemporary, the 'Brighton Belle', survived into the 1970s. Like the 'Golden Arrow' vehicles, the 15 Pullmans were refurbished and turned out in corporate blue and grey in the winter of 1969/70. Many of us welcomed this if it meant the survival of the 'Belle', even though we shuddered at its appearance.

However, despite what must have been an expensive modernisation programme - which included replacing the number stencils with a roller-blind, a particularly pointless exercise as the only number it normally needed was 4, Victoria to Brighton non-stop - the train's time was nearly up. With the introduction of the CIGs and BIGs, the non-stop time between Victoria and Brighton was cut to 55 minutes. The 'Belle' had plenty of power to cope with this, but inevitably its constant rough riding grew rougher. The decision was eventually taken to withdraw it, and it made its last run on 30 September 1972.

I interviewed the Manager of the Central Division a few months earlier on behalf of Railway World, and discovered that it was largely sentiment rather than customers that had kept the 'Belle' running in its last few years. Many of us feel that labour-saving has gone too far on BR in the 1990s, but the issue has been with us for a very long time. Even 20 years ago, when ticket collectors were not a threatened species, the Southern was thought to be overstaffed.

The 'Belle' required a pool of no fewer than 35 attendants, 14 of whom were on duty at any one time. However, most of the passengers had little use for the Pullman's all but 40-year-old splendours, merely requiring a seat and a fast, safe run to Brighton. For instance, only 44 full breakfasts were served daily in an average month on the 9.25 am out of Brighton.

Perhaps the clinching argument was that the 'Belle' had always been somewhat rough riding and it could not be denied that the new CIG and BIG units were much superior in this respect.

The ten-car train, headed by unit No 3051, arrives at Victoria in the spring of 1969. The names of the cars have disappeared - even the legend 'Pullman' has disappeared, being replaced by 'Brighton Belle' along the lower panels of each car.

No 3051 is seen again with motor brake 2nd Class car No 288 (originally No 88) leading, leaving the sidings at Lover's Walk, Brighton, beside rows of 2BILs and 2HALs.

So famous was the 'Brighton Belle' that all 15 carriages were almost immediately bought for preservation. Since then their fate has been varied. Two which are still electrically hauled are 'Doris' and 'Vera' (see page 50), which work in the Venice-Simplon-Orient Express. Two of the motor cars are presently at Brighton, in the former Pullman Car Company Works at Preston Park, whilst others

have gone far from home, many miles from the third rail.

One of them, No 88, has been bought for the VSOE and will operate as a driving trailer. Electrically hauled, restored to its traditional livery and working on the third rail with its erstwhile companions 'Vera' and 'Audrey', it will come as near as most of us would ever have dared hope to recreating the 'Brighton Belle'.

In this view, motor car No 90 is seen at the Nene Valley Railway.

Inevitably those residing on preserved railways find themselves steam hauled. Motor car No 88 departs from Herston Halt during its stay on the Swanage Railway in 1986.

Withdrawal of the 2HALs took place at the same time as the 2BILs, and the last duties of both types were along the Sussex coast. 2HAL No 2687 approaches Hastings at the beginning of its run from Ore to Brighton in July 1969.

As with all elderly Southern stock, curious things happened to various vehicles from 2HAL units in their last months of passenger service. In 1969 four HAL motor coaches and four spare Bulleid suburban trailers were used to create two 4SUB units. One of these, No 4132, is seen at London Bridge in 1970. In the background is one of the original 4SUBs of the 4101-9 series; it can be seen how closely the motor coach ends resembled those of the HALs.

Various 2HAL vehicles were rebuilt for departmental service. Stores unit No 023 is seen passing Coulsdon North on 16 July 1983. *Alex Dasi-Sutton*

The withdrawal of the 2BILs and 2HALs left a handful of 4CORs as the final survivors of the Southern Railway's main-line electric multiple units. They had disappeared from their original haunts on the Waterloo-Portsmouth and Mid-Sussex routes some time earlier and, like the BILs and HALs, ended their days on stopping services between Brighton, Seaford, Eastbourne, Hastings and Ore. The last of them was withdrawn on 2 October 1972 and with them ended a significant chapter in British railway history.

In 1933 the stock provided for the new Brighton line electric service had been to the very latest designs, which had also been the case for the subsequent extensions to Eastbourne, Hastings, Littlehampton, Bognor and Portsmouth. If not the equal of the special vehicles built by the GWR, LMS and LNER for the centenary 'Cornish Riviera' and the streamliners, Southern Electric express carriages were as good as any to be found in normal main-line service.

Sadly, by the 1970s this was no longer so. Mark 2 carriages had been introduced with the LMR electrification in 1966, air-conditioned vehicles went into production for the WR, LMR and ER in 1971, and by 1976 HSTs with their superb Mark 3 carriages were coming into service, first on the Western Region, then for the East Coast. It seemed as though the Southern Electric main-line network was to be regarded as little more than a glorified outer suburban system worked exclusively by various out-moded Mark 1 designs.

No 3160 leaves Eastbourne for Ore in the summer of 1972. This was one of ten units formed in the spring of 1966 with former 4RES motor cars flanking a 2nd and a composite from either a PUL or a PAN unit. The origin of the trailer carriages is given away by their louvred doors.

2HAPs replaced the post-war 2HALs on the Gatwick Airport-Victoria services; BR-type No 6049 is seen here in June 1970 coupled to an SR-type unit - which in many respects closely resembled a post-war HAL - and a 4VEP.

A most curious stop-gap arrangement which brought a 2BIL unit to the then non-electrified Oxted line is seen here approaching South Croydon in the summer of 1967. This is 7TC unit No 701. The first and last carriages are the former 2BIL No 2006, while the other five are elderly Bulleid suburban vehicles which originally worked with pre-Grouping 3SUBs. One of them actually had its 1st Class compartments used as such, although it never had before. The motive power is a Birmingham RC&W Type 3 Bo-Bo diesel-electric, which came to be better known as a 'Crompton' or Class '33'; the train is the 17.20 London Bridge to Tunbridge Wells West. The unit was disbanded the following winter and the 2BIL vehicles broken up.

The mid-1970s was a period of quiet reflection on the Southern Electric main lines. The old order had gone, just about everything now bore, or soon would bear, the standard blue and grey livery except for suburban units, and in some ways we were back to the situation of the 1950s when the Southern Electric went its own idiosyncratic way, paying little heed to what the rest of BR was doing. However, the revolution which would at last bring Southern EMUs into the latter part of the 20th century was about to happen. In 1971 the prototypes of the first sliding-door suburban units appeared.

Designated 4PEPs, No 4002, the second of these four-coach units, stands in Clapham Yard (extreme right) in the summer of 1988 alongside a fascinating collection of carriages which includes a former Southern Railway Maunsell Inspection Saloon, a BR Mark 1 sleeper (goodness knows what that was doing on the Southern), Class '438' 4TC No 8024 (formerly 424), and three buffet cars from withdrawn 4REP units.

The PEPs were the forerunners of generations of EMUs which would work suburban traffic, not just on the Southern but all over the electrified lines of BR. They would also have a great influence on electric units built for long-distance work on the Southern. But not yet. The very last service on BR to sport traditional carriage headboards was the Channel Island Boat Train, as seen here on an early BR Mark 2 1st in the summer of 1977.

A Class '73' leaves the Western Docks for Waterloo with a rake of BR Mark 1s in May 1984 with passengers off the *Norway*, the former *France*. A short while later it passed an incoming train with passengers for the QE2, a rare event indeed, for by that date weeks would go by without sight or sound of a passenger train in Southampton Docks, and boat trains, once a significant element in the passenger traffic of the Southern, were in steady decline through the 1970s and '80s. The Channel Islands service lasted until the collapse of the Sealink services from Weymouth at the end of the 1985 summer season. There remains some demand at Southampton for QE2 and other cruise-liner passengers, although this is minimal compared with the great days which ended in the 1960s.

Dover was now on its way to becoming the busiest passenger port in the world. Most of this traffic came and went by road, but many thousands of cross-Channel passengers still travelled by train. Two 4CEPs stand in the sidings at Dover Marine in July 1984 dwarfed by the funnel of a ferry.

Only on the Eastern Section were boat trains still a familiar sight. A 13-coach train (three 4CEPs and a motor luggage van) from Victoria, having just reversed, heads down the incline towards Folkestone Harbour in the summer of 1972.

9 Refurbishment: 1979-87

By the late 1970s the CEPs and BEPs were approaching their 20th birthday and were distinctly old-fashioned. Being the Southern, no one seriously considered building new stock. Instead, an extensive rebuilding programme was sanctioned, following the experimental refurbishment of No 7153 at Eastleigh in 1975. Several BR Works far away from Southern Electric metals had been involved in the production of Southern EMUs during the 1960s and '70s, so it was not perhaps very surprising that Swindon was awarded the contract for the CEP/BEP programme.

The appearance and the layout of the units was changed considerably, and for the better. The two guard's/luggage compartments at either end of the units were abolished, to be replaced by one in the trailer composite. Hopper-type window ventilators were fitted into the double-glazed windows, inverters, fluorescent lighting, public address equipment, up-to-date seating and new gangway connections were further improvements. The riding of the CEPs and BEPs had left much to be desired; later ones had non-powered Commonwealth bogies and these were now fitted to all units, although the original motor bogies were retained. This was an improvement, although not so marked that the CEPs could equal the comforts of locomotive-hauled stock.

CEP/BEP refurbishment work approaches completion inside the former GWR Works at Swindon in 1979.

For a short while Swindon turned out units with six-figure numbers which began with 411, the new class designation, as seen here on unit 411508, but this was soon abandoned and all units are now numbered between 1500 and 1621.

Only a small number of the buffet bars, seven in all, were rebuilt. The remainder were replaced by former locomotive-hauled open 2nds and no catering cars would in future normally operate on the Eastern Section. From now on refreshments would be provided by mobile trolleys - well, it was better than nothing. The seven remaining 4BEPs were sent to work the Waterloo-Portsmouth express services, usually flanked by two 4CIG units. No 2306 is seen at Portsmouth Harbour on 3 September 1991; the buffet car is the second vehicle.

With the withdrawal of the 'Golden Arrow' on 30 September 1972, Pullmans, which had for long been a more familiar sight on Southern metals than on any other part of Britain's rail network, were no more - the best one could hope to find was the occasional visitor from elsewhere. One of the Metro-Cammell cars of 1960, demoted to an ordinary 1st and used on the 'Hook Continental' between Parkstone Quay and Liverpool Street, No E353E, is seen here in the sidings at Clapham Junction on 19 September 1980, shortly before passing to the Steam Locomotive Operators Association who restored it to its original chocolate and cream livery.

And then, surprise, surprise, the Pullmans returned. In May 1982 the ultra-luxurious, hyper-ultra-expensive Venice-Simplon-Orient Express was inaugurated. A variety of cars dating from between 1925 and 1952 were restored. One of the oldest, 'Minerva', built by the Midland RC&W company in 1927, is seen with attendants waiting at Folkestone Harbour at Easter 1987.

Earlier that day two of the Wagon Lits vehicles of the connecting mainland Europe VSOE are seen at Boulogne Maritime.

Preservation was in the air throughout the 1980s, particularly of non-steam power which until then had been very much of minority interest. 4SUB No 4732, restored to its original green livery and hauled by the distinctive former Metropolitan Railway 1,200 hp Bo-Bo locomotive No 12 *Sarah Siddons* of 1920, passes East Croydon on a special run from Selhurst to Brighton on 15 July 1983. *John Scrace*

Since the opening of the London to Brighton line on 20 September 1841 the principal trains had always been the through expresses. But changing times and patterns of travel and the pre-eminence of the airliner for long-distance travel eventually brought this to an end. Gatwick Airport, with its terminal extending across the railway tracks, was steadily generating more and more traffic for British Rail.

In the summer of 1963 I worked as a porter at Gatwick Airport station and although the airport was only a fraction of the size it is now, there was plenty of business, lots of tanned ladies in pink outfits and large, plastic picture hats, youths in flares, and British United Airways hostesses in tight skirts which my fellow student and porter Noel attempted to chat up with varying degrees of success.

The great majority of the passengers were travelling between Benidorm, Majorca and Victoria and were conveyed in Viscounts, BAC 111s and post-war 2HALs. The few who headed south by train were offered a variety of destinations. One set in particular is engraved on my memory. Although I love poetry I can scarcely remember a line of anything, but

> 'Three Bridges, Balcombe,
> Haywards Heath, Wivelsfield,
> Burgess Hill, Hassocks,
> Preston Park and Brighton'

rolls off my tongue as trippingly as the Lord's Prayer. Gatwick Airport station possessed a recording of a suave BBC-type voice for almost all possible permutations of routes and destinations. However, at quiet times when those in authority were upstairs drinking tea and the elderly driver who shunted the HALs from one platform to another was filling in an application form for transfer to Boeing 707s, we student porters would daringly take the microphone ourselves. The Mid-Sussex line had some nice rhythms. 'Billinghurst and Pullborough' could well have provided the core of a Betjeman masterpiece, but all stations to Brighton was our favourite.

Despite our efforts, traffic through Gatwick increased throughout the 1960s and '70s and in 1984 the 'Gatwick Express' took to the tracks. Refurbished Mark 2F carriages brought air-conditioning to the Southern for the first time and, powered by Class '73s' at one end with a former HAP motor coach converted to a guard's luggage van with a driving cab at the other, the Class '488' Gatwick Expresses in Inter-City livery run every quarter of an hour non-stop to and from Victoria.

An up 'Gatwick Express' passing Coulsdon North in June 1991.

The 'Gatwick Expresses' are based at Stewarts Lane. A Class '73' and trailer 1st/Standard No 72646 of unit No 8319 in the depot in August 1988 with a Class '411' 4CEP in the background.

In 1982 the more or less permanent coupling of pairs of 2HAPs was officially recognised by re-classification to 4CAP, the 'C' standing for Coastway as they were employed along the coast east and west from Brighton. They lost their 1st Class accommodation, but this was restored when the units subsequently moved eastwards. Two of these 4CAPs (Class '413'), Nos 3212/3208, pass Petts Wood forming the 09.00 Charing Cross-Ashford train on 8 August 1987. *David Brown*

Right A few months before the completion of the Hastings line electrification, a Charing Cross train with 6L Class '202' DEMU No 1018 in the rear sends a fine cloud of oily pollution into the clear Kentish morning air as it leaves Tonbridge passing 4VEP No 7862 waiting on the through road.

Below Rush-hour Oxted line services feature elderly Southern Railway-type 2EPBs. No 6317, built in 1959 on 1934/6-built underframes, brings up the rear behind a 4VEP (Class '423') at Hurst Green on a Victoria-East Grinstead train on 16 April 1992.

When the second phase of the Kent Coast electrification scheme was completed in 1969, Tonbridge remained a centre of diesel multiple unit operation. The 'Tadpoles' worked westwards to Redhill and Reading, the 3D and 3H units to Tunbridge Wells West and thence to Uckfield and Oxted, whilst the earliest of them all, the Hastings six-car units, continued to monopolise all passenger workings on that line between London and the Sussex coast. Eventually the problems of the tunnels which resulted in the building of excessively narrow carriages especially for this line were resolved by singling the track through them, and in 1986 electrification arrived.

Ever since Southern Railway days there had been promises to electrify the Oxted line. On several occasions hopes had risen, only to be dashed, and since the early 1960s the inhabitants of the green and pleasant lands served by the line had had to put up with not very comfortable three-car DEMUs.

Electrification arrived at last on Sunday 27 September 1987, although the branch from Oxted to Uckfield remained in the hands of diesels, the Eridge to Tunbridge Wells West line was closed and of course the network south of Uckfield and East Grinstead had long disappeared (except for the Bluebell Railway which operates between Sheffield Park and Horsted Keynes and was then about to receive permission to extend to East Grinstead), but it was better than nothing.

10 'Wessex Electrics' and Thameslink: 1987-89

Network SouthEast was launched on 10 June 1986, and was a very much more high profile renaming of London and South East, created in 1982. Incorporating all of Southern Electric, plus former Eastern, London Midland and Western Region lines radiating from London to Southend, Clacton, Huntingdon, Bedford, Banbury, Bedwyn and the former LSWR main line to Exeter, it introduced a new, initially somewhat startling red, white and blue livery. Carnaby Street had gone psychedelic in the 1960s when the 4CIGs were bright young things, but it took the best part of 30 years for rainbow hues to spread the mile or so down Regent Street and across Trafalgar Square and St James's Park to reach their vintage contours.

London and South East had introduced a two-tone brown and orange colour scheme for main-line trains, which had only limited application, the principal recipients being the Kent Coast 4CEPs. Inevitably the colours soon became known as 'Jaffa cake'. It was a rather pleasing livery and is seen here adorning a boat train about to depart from Victoria in the summer of 1989 with Class '419' DMLV No 9001 in the rear. These interesting vehicles were built in 1969 and fitted with traction batteries for working over non-electrified lines on the quaysides at Dover and Folkestone.

Multi-coloured Network SouthEast 4CIG No 1216 speeds through the New Forest near Beaulieu Road in the spring of 1991 on a Wareham to Portsmouth Harbour working.

After years of hesitation and even threats of closure (would you believe it?), or at best singling, common sense prevailed and work began at the end of 1986 on the electrification of the Bournemouth to Weymouth line. A Weymouth-bound train composed of a 4TC, Class '491', which has worked from Waterloo coupled to a 4REP, Class '432', approaches Wareham in May 1987 behind a Class '33' diesel-electric locomotive which replaced the REP at Bournemouth; on either side are engineering trains loaded with electric cables. The third rail is partly in place.

Several years before the third rail reached Weymouth, 4SUB Class '405' No 4687 appeared in the sidings there; surely this wasn't going to be provided for we simple Dorset folk to journey all the way to the Big Smoke? However, as can be seen by its condition its passenger-carrying days were over - it had been withdrawn in May 1983, and served at Weymouth as an exercise unit for the emergency services.

The Weymouth electrification was inaugurated with the summer 1988 timetable. Wareham had its service of one passenger train an hour in each direction doubled with the extension of the stopping service which hitherto had terminated at Bournemouth. Two 4VEPs are seen on the opening day, No 3019 bound for Weymouth, No 3001 arriving from that town.

The 4REPs began to be withdrawn before the new units, which incorporated 4REP traction motors, entered service, and Class '73s' were drafted into the breach, often working in pairs and hauling hybrid units which incorporated former 4REP buffet cars. Nos 73131 *County of Surrey* and 73103 pause at Clapham Junction with a Weymouth to Waterloo express in October 1987.

The elderly 4VEPs were intended to work stopping services, but delays in the delivery of the new express units saw them pressed into emergency long-distance work. Nevertheless the express units were certainly worth waiting for. Classified '442', they are better known as the 'Wessex Electrics'. These superb units were a quantum leap forward in Southern EMU design.

The first 'Wessex Electric', No 2401, departs from Wareham on 16 May 1988 forming the inaugural working of the 17.15 Waterloo to Weymouth 'Royal Wessex', a welcome revival of a name which had disappeared with steam. Earlier that year I had travelled on the record-breaking run of Thursday 11 April when two Class '442' units made the fastest ever non-stop journey between Waterloo and Weymouth in 1 hour, 59 minutes, 24 seconds.

An Open Day was held at Bournemouth depot that summer. Crowds are queuing to sample the delights of a brand new 'Wessex Electric', whilst in the background are a Class '73', a '47' and the preserved 4SUB No 4732.

Top left Units Nos 2412 and 2403 at Bournemouth in the summer of 1991, having just arrived from Waterloo. The introduction of the 'Wessex Electrics' meant that for the first time since the 1930s the Southern could boast express stock equal to that found anywhere else in Britain. It was even possible to partake of refreshments whilst travelling alongside the water meadows of the Piddle between Wareham and Wool, if you were very quick - what joy! Air-conditioned and with automatic doors (troublesome at first), the 'Wessex Electrics' rode superbly, a vast improvement on their 4REP predecessors. Visually they at last got away from the more or less flat-ended, cut-out-two-windows-and-stick-on-a-corridor-connection school of design, and as a consequence are just about the best-looking multiple units to be found anywhere in Europe.

Centre left The 10.32 Waterloo-Weymouth 'Wessex Electric' rushes down the bank from Bincombe tunnel on the approach to Weymouth on 25 April 1992.

Bottom left A Waterloo-Poole semi-fast 'Wessex Electric' hurries to get ahead of an April storm at Battledown in the spring of 1992.

Below The 16.32 Waterloo-Weymouth 'Wessex Electric' leaves Wareham on 20 April 1992.

One of the worst accidents on BR for many years occurred between Earlsfield and Clapham Junction on 12 December 1988. The 06.30 Bournemouth to Waterloo crashed into the back of the 07.18 Basingstoke to Waterloo which had stopped because of faulty signals. A third electric train, the 08.03 Waterloo to Haslemere empties, hit the wreckage. Thirty-two passengers and two railwaymen, all in the front section of the Bournemouth train, 4REP No 2003, died. The remains of one of No 2003's carriages is partially reassembled in East Wimbledon depot for the subsequent enquiry. *Colin Marsden*

No 73201 *Broadlands*, a favourite for state occasions, takes the Quarry line on 12 July 1988 bringing the President of Turkey to meet the Queen at Victoria. The combination of a station within the airport and the proximity of Victoria station to Buckingham Palace - the side entrance is actually in Buckingham Palace Road, a pretty superior address for anyone's back gate - has ensured that most state visitors arrive at Gatwick and travel thence by train to the capital. *John Scrace*

The most revolutionary change on the Brighton line since electrification took place on 16 May 1988 when Thameslink opened. The long-disused Snow Hill tunnel between the former Great Northern Railway at Farringdon and Blackfriars, which had not seen regular passenger services since Edwardian times, was relaid and 86 four-car units, Class '319', were built to work between Bedford, on the former Midland Railway main line, and Wimbledon, Sevenoaks, Gatwick Airport and Brighton. And perhaps because they worked beyond Southern territory they really were brand new. The '319s' are dual-fitted, changing from 25kV 50Hz ac overhead at Farringdon, where the pantographs are retracted and 750V dc third rail is used for the Southern Region section of their journey. Thameslink proved instantly popular and 26 further units of Class '319/1', with 1st Class accommodation for Brighton commuter traffic, were built in 1990. On 27 July 1991 two Class '319s' established a fastest ever time between Victoria and Brighton of 39 minutes, 38 seconds.

A number of Thameslink services carry buffet trolleys and, although strictly speaking they are outer suburban units, the '319s' are considerably more comfortable than the elderly and now rather shabby CIG and BIG express units.

No 319023 stands at Brighton station in the autumn of 1988, ready to depart with a Thameslink service for Bedford.

No 319165 at Farringdon on 9 November 1991 about to change from third rail to overhead collection. On the right a Metropolitan line train from Amersham to Baker Street is arriving.

Thameslink above the Thames - No 319169 at Blackfriars, with the Embankment and the river beyond, on a Bedford to Gatwick Airport working on 4 January 1992.

11 Present and future: the 1990s

The 1990s were only five months old when yet another section of the ever-dwindling non-electrified Southern network succumbed to the third rail. This was the coast line from Southampton to Portsmouth (strictly speaking St Denys to Portcreek Junction), together with the Eastleigh to Fareham connection. The third rail now stretched all along the Dorset, Hampshire and Sussex coasts from Weymouth to Ore. As with the Tonbridge to Hastings and the Oxted schemes, no new stock was needed, but a considerable restructuring of services saw the lucky citizens of Fareham receive a regular service to and from London for the first time ever, a semi-fast running between Waterloo, Basingstoke, Eastleigh, Fareham and Portsmouth & Southsea in each direction every hour, whilst the Wareham to Southampton stopping service was extended to Portsmouth Harbour.

A 4VEP heading for Wareham is seen amidst the plethora of splendidly maintained Victorian ironwork of St Denys station in May 1991.

A number of 4CIGs (Class '421') were modified so as to be capable of running at up to 100 mph and facelifted internally to work the fastest Portsmouth line services. Known as the 'Greyhounds', they were distinguished by black areas above the numbers. 'Greyhound' No 1303 pulls out of Clapham Junction for Waterloo on 4 January 1992, while to the left in the sidings is No 410, one of two 4TC trailer units repainted at the end of 1991 into more or less original 'Rail blue' livery and refurbished at a cost of £15,000 for charter work. The units are based at Bournemouth depot.

An uprated 4CIG passes Battledown on a Portsmouth-Waterloo working on 15 April 1992.

Since the summer of 1992 Class '442s' have worked Portsmouth-Waterloo expresses. One was photographed at Portsmouth Harbour on 27 July 1992.

Semaphore signals had been gradually disappearing throughout the 1980s - they were to be seen in some numbers between Hove and Bognor until almost the end of the decade - but a few pockets remained when the last decade of the 20th century opened. Some were to be found with their accompanying boxes along the picturesque Stour Valley line between Canterbury and Ashford at the end of 1991. Here 4CEP No 1567 pulls out under Canterbury West box bound for Minster and Ramsgate.

In the 1990s the Mid-Sussex line is the last section of the main-line Southern Electric network where semaphores are almost universal. This is Pulborough on 27 July 1992.

In January 1990 the original Holborn Viaduct station closed, being replaced by an underground Thameslink station. Shortly afterwards the famous - but it has to be admitted not very pretty - bridge which carried trains across Ludgate Circus was demolished, and for the first time for 116 years it was possible to have a clear view down Fleet Street to St Paul's Cathedral. On the evening of 26 January 1990 4CEP No 1605 heads the last train out of Holborn Viaduct. *Colin Marsden*

Far and away the most exciting development ever to hit Southern Electric is the Channel Tunnel. Whether any reader will live long enough to see the full completion of the network on this side of the Channel is, however, to be doubted. . . Never mind - at the time of writing the tunnel itself looks like being ready for trains running between Waterloo, Paris and Brussels by the winter of 1993.

The working N gauge model of the Folkestone terminal, seen under construction below, on display at the Channel Tunnel exhibition centre at Cheriton, Folkestone.

Mainland Europe locomotives could be seen at work at the Channel Tunnel terminus at Folkestone by the summer of 1991 - but they had to come by sea. Four former Deutsche Bundesbahn '211' Class diesel-hydraulics were bought for use on construction work trains and one is seen here on 6 July of that year.

Above Colourfully mixed motive power for an Engineers train at the Channel Tunnel works, Battersea, in June 1992.

Below On 14 July 1992 the last of 44 trains carrying long-welded rail for the Channel Tunnel from British Steel Track Products, Workington, arrives at the tunnel portal at Cheriton, hauled by RFS Class '20' No 2018. *Brian Morrison*

Top right Waterloo, January 1991. Seen amongst the bicycles is (from the left) Class '421/2' CIG No 1211 (with barely discernible number applied below the cab window, an unfortunate practice which soon ceased when someone in authority realised that numbers were meant to be legible), Class '423/0' 4VEP No 3110, and the Channel Tunnel test train, former 4TC No 8007 in departmental livery.

Centre right The Channel Tunnel test train, behind a Class '73' and a Class '33', passes Battledown on its way to Eastleigh on 15 April 1992.

Bottom right The shape of things to come - 'Networker' units, delivered to Network SouthEast, at Clapham Junction on 20 July 1992.

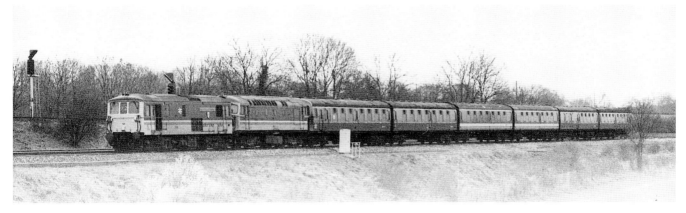

Work in progress at Waterloo in July 1991.

Further views of Waterloo in February 1992 (*above*) and July 1992 (*left*).

Scheduled to finish when the Channel Tunnel opened, continuing losses by Stena Sealink forced the premature closures of the Folkestone to Boulogne ferry service at the end of 1991. Here is *Stena Horsa* alongside the quay at Folkestone on 29 December of that year.

Looking from the deck of the *Stena Horsa* towards the viaduct which carries the main line across the town.

To mark the closure of the ferry service, Network SouthEast and the Southern Electric Group organised a series of runs from Ashford down the harbour branch to the quay at Folkestone in the pioneer 4EPB unit No 5001, restored to its original green livery. It is seen here pausing at Sandling, one time junction for the Hythe branch, on 29 December 1991.

The vintage SECR Saxby & Farmer signal box at Folkestone Harbour station and two 4CEPs pulling out on a boat train frame No 5001 at the platform.

In the summer of 1991 the Isle of Wight Steam Railway, with the active help of Network SouthEast, completed its extension eastwards to Smallbrook Junction, where the Shanklin and Cowes lines used to diverge, and a new station was built there, served by both steam and electric trains. '02' Class 0-4-4T No 24 *Calbourne* runs around its train whilst Class '483' No 008 pulls in on its way to Shanklin.

It was in 1989 that the ancient former London Transport tube trains on the Isle of Wight began to be replaced by – wait for it – ancient former London Transport tube trains; only they weren't quite as ancient as their predecessors. The '483s' date from 1938, and despite their Network SouthEast livery, which suits them rather well, no one is fooled into taking them for anything other than the antiques they are, especially when they lurch around the bends outside Ryde St Johns.

Inside a Class '483'.

Two Class '483s' seen at St Johns on 3 September 1991. The station has the air of belonging to another era with its decorative awning, semaphore signal, and former SECR signal box.

1991 was the 150th anniversary of the opening of the London to Brighton line, and the culmination of the celebrations took place over the weekend of 21-22 September at Brighton itself. The VSOE train of restored Pullmans, including former 'Brighton Belle' vehicles 'Vera' and 'Audrey', is seen approaching Brighton with the 09.00 special from Victoria, hauled by Class '73/1' No 73101 *Brighton Evening Argus*, and passing a number of Lover's Walk Depot Open Day exhibits, on the Saturday morning. *Brian Morrison*

Remarkable scenes took place on the Sunday when Lover's Walk was thrown open to the public. In this panoramic view there is not a Southern electric in sight, for the first time in almost 60 years. From left to right are former LB&SCR locos 0-4-2 *Gladstone* and 'Terrier' 0-6-0T *Stepney*, and BR Standard '4MT' 2-6-4T No 80080, all built at Brighton Works; SR 'King Arthur' 'N15' 4-6-0 No 777 *Sir Lamiel*, representing a class which once used to haul the 'Southern Belle'; the pioneer BR Standard '7MT' 'Pacific' No 70000 *Britannia*; and a final Brighton-built locomotive, Bulleid 'Pacific' No 34027 *Taw Valley*.

The 4VEP which operated the shuttle from Lover's Walk to Brighton station passes *Gladstone* and *Stepney*.

Above Pullman-liveried No 73101 *Brighton Evening Argus* at the head of the 4VEP shuttle inside the depot.

Below EMU visitors from afar. Preserved LNER-design Class '306' No 017, built in 1949 from the Liverpool Street to Shenfield services, and Glasgow area Class '303' No 048, built in 1960, both restored to their original liveries, stand alongside SR Class '419' motor luggage van No 9004.

Above right A link with the days of the Brighton overhead electrics. The AC motor vans were converted to bogie goods brake-vans and many of **a** further series to the same design, built new in the 1930s, are still in use. One is seen here at the Brighton Open Day, restored to Southern Railway livery.

Below right Preserved 4COR No 3142, belonging to the Southern Electric Group, and preserved 2BIL No 2090, part of the National Collection.

Arundel. An unpretentious mid-Victorian brick house, dating from 1863, looking across the Arun to the grandeur of the castle and the Roman Catholic cathedral perched on the hillside.

Three Bridges. LB&SCR Victorian engraved glass alongside Network SouthEast 1980s graphic design.

Portsmouth & Southsea. Florid Victoriana at its most confident. Built in 1876, there are echoes, particularly in its roof line, of the Brighton side of Victoria.

Rowlands Castle. There's an interesting story behind the pleasantly unpretentious down-side building. As part of the recent speed-up of Portsmouth-Waterloo services the curve through Rowlands Castle was eased. The canopy on the down side would have fouled the track and British Rail originally intended to demolish the entire building and replace it with a cheap and nasty 'bus shelter'. Various objections were raised and in the end Dean Clark, Head of the Historic Building Bureau of the Planning Department of Hampshire County Council, and his son, Tom, came up with a plan which involved moving the canopy back, providing fresh columns, of the correct vintage and design brought in from elsewhere, constructing new valancing and generally restoring the building. A former shipwright employed by BR constructed embellishments for the windows. The money came from Network SouthEast, the BR Heritage Trust and Hampshire County Council, and all in all Rowlands Castle provides a perfect example in miniature of what can be done to preserve our rich and diverse railway architectural heritage.

Faversham. Patterns of London, Chatham & Dover ironwork, glass and wooden valancing.

Dover Western Docks. The former Marine station, 'Gateway to the Continent', opened by the SECR in 1915.

Richmond, a handsome Southern Railway rebuilding completed in 1937. *National Railway Museum, York*

Chichester. Completed in 1961, this is pure post-Festival of Britain in every detail. One hopes that in this cathedral city where there is such concern for architecture no 'modernisation' will be allowed to spoil the purity of this splendid period piece.

Modern image. A collection of luggage trolleys at Weymouth. The original GWR station, or what was left of it, was demolished and a more modern, but attractive, new one opened in July 1986.

13 Network Day: A Southern Electric day out

We're going to end with a day out on the Southern Electric. We all like days out, and Network SouthEast, recognising this, has for several years arranged that anyone who possesses a Network Card can travel as much of the network as they like for little more than a nominal sum once each year. This is a sort of thank you for patronising Network SouthEast all the rest of the year. What's that I hear? Some people regard any not absolutely necessary trip on Network SouthEast a penance? No, that's unkind!

They don't have Network Days in the middle of August, they're not that altruistic; the one we're all going on was on the second Saturday in November 1991. It will cost us a fiver, plus 80p for an underground ticket and another couple of pounds for various cups of tea. We are taking our own lunch and snacks - the recession is still with us and money doesn't grow on trees.

Our journey begins on the 06.40 Poole to Manchester. Not an electric train at all, admittedly, at least not until it gets to Coventry and by then it's nothing to do with the Southern. But our first destination is Reading and it's third rail practically all the way. Class '47' No 47812, very clean in InterCity livery with a rake of six matching air-conditioned Mark 2s and a passenger brake, gets away on time just as a faint lightening in the eastern sky tells us that dawn is breaking.

Most of the seats have reserved labels, but few of them are occupied. The sun rises over the New Forest, Southampton Docks are unusually busy - a '47' is shunting at the container terminal with a ship from the Far East unloading alongside, there's another big vessel in dry dock and P&O's *Canberra* in the Western Docks. A former Class '33', now No 83301, is attached to the Channel Tunnel test train at Eastleigh, standing in front of a row of dead Oxted DEMUs. Now the sun is up, the sky a clear blue.

We leave Southern Electric at Basingstoke, but at Reading we're back, briefly, in Southern Electric territory; the 08.44 to Waterloo, 4VEP No 3520, pulls out and takes itself off down the hill on to the Southern proper. Meanwhile we board the 09.55 HST for Paddington. It's packed but we find a seat next to a lady reading the *Guardian* and behind a couple of Welshmen. Snatches of conversation drift back.

'Makes you wonder where all these people are going.'

'I see him Wednesday in Merthyr.'

Could he be referring to Neil Kinnock? Probably not.

Why are we going to Paddington? Well, as it happens No 5029 *Nunney Castle*, the first ex-GWR 'Castle' to be seen on a main-line express there for over 20 years, is about to depart for Stratford upon Avon. Magnificent sight, sun gleaming on Brunswick green paintwork, brass and copperwork, smoke and steam aplenty.

That duty done, we take the Inner Circle to Farringdon, cross the platform to Thameslink, and have a look at where the overhead gives way to the third rail. The 10.38 to Sevenoaks, No 319042, pulls in and we board. Very nice trains, much better than a lot of Southern main-line stock.

A number of wolf cubs get out at Citylink St Pauls, going to the Lord Mayor's Show no doubt. I never used to miss that - going with school friends meant I was able to travel up to London Bridge in a 4LAV from East Croydon rather than the usual 4SUB from Thornton Heath. The last time we took our three young sons, the presenters from *Blue Peter* were taking part, and oldest son William asked how they had managed to get out of the TV set. As he's now studying Philosophy at Bristol University I dare say he's worked out the answer.

We emerge back into daylight at Blackfriars and negotiate inner suburbia, Del Boy territory, pass the Prince (Uncle?) Albert and Camberwell bus garage, and overtake a Routemaster on the 36.

Beyond Loughborough Junction the scenery becomes surprisingly rural with the rich autumn colours of Ruskin Park. In a short tunnel I am diverted by a conversation further down the carriage.

'He said to me, Yousif got 100 per cent, dead queer, Sir, he never used a calculator, closed his eyes, just looked up into the sky, then wrote down the answer.'

Before I can follow this up we're at Peckham Rye, where we get out. A Class '33', very natty in two shades of grey, dashes past on the South Eastern main line, then Class '455' No 5820 pulls in complete with young lady in off-the-shoulder furry jumper. Must be frozen - it's pretty nippy out today. Above the rooftops St Paul's gleams in a patch of sunlight, and soon we arrive at London Bridge.

Cross over to the Eastern side where there's time for a cup of tea and the opportunity to observe the venerable 4EPBs - some looking like mutton dressed as lamb with Network stripes wrapped around their distinctive toplights - going about their business, remarkable antiques alongside the Thameslink '319s' and the brand-new South London line '456s'.

We are now off to Faversham, and in comes the 11.46 which should take us to Gillingham, but won't. It's the weekend, so Network SouthEast is having a dig up in the Medway Towns and we will have to resort to a bus from Stroud. Once the Charing Cross to Gillingham service was considered long-distance and was operated by 2HALs and later 2HAPs. Not any more. Today the 40-year-old suburban 4EPBs have the pleasure, so we find ourselves sitting in the front compartment of Network-liveried 5426, having climbed in over a young citizen in his buggy.

We note that Lewisham is to have a 'boot sale this Sunday', then a neatly executed piece of graffiti on a yellow-grey brick wall advises travellers 'Be cool - but care', while a truly splendid mural decorates the end of a terrace by Charlton station. 'Charlton Lane Crossing' is unexpected, a genuine SECR single-storey box still fully operational.

Being in the nature of a semi-fast we shoot through Woolwich Dockyard and several other stations without stopping. A most surprising sight is a pony and trap with two up trotting purposely towards a concrete high-rise block of flats just before Abbey Wood. Baby, buggy, mum and dad get out here.

No 5246 accelerates away rapidly and fairly bounces past dozens more EPBs taking the weekend off at Slade Green depot. We draw into Dartford where there is a nice view of the pond and the gasworks. A great many passengers get out and a good few get in.

The Thames has been in view for several miles and continues to be - the new Dartford road bridge looks supremely elegant, unlike Essex man who is probably even now pouring across. A Balt-Orient Line CS container vessel is making its way upstream. The marshes beyond Gravesend evoke memories of Charles Dickens, *Great Expectations*, and the delicious Jean Simmons. We halt briefly at Hoo Junction Staff Halt,

just long enough to note Nos 56059, 09005, 33042 and 73134 in the sidings.

We arrive at Stroud at 12.43, 57 minutes after leaving London Bridge, my longest journey ever in almost 40 years of spasmodic EPB travel. Latest predictions suggest that there's time for a good many more before they expire.

A very grand Mercedes-Berkhof coach is waiting in the station yard. Vastly more luxurious than any EPB, this in no way compensates for a journey which by train would have taken 10 minutes including stops at Rochester and Chatham stations, occupying, with the same number of stops, 33 minutes by road. Nos 33052 *Ashford* and 33012, both in old all-blue livery, are chuntering away to themselves in Gillingham station, in charge of a rake of ballast wagons. In the distance a couple of 4EPBs can be seen in the siding.

Our train, two 4VEPs, draws in to form the 13.49 all stations to Ramsgate. As we pull out past the depot there would be excellent views of the Medway estuary were it not for unit No 3449's dirty windows, which, with the sun reflecting off them, exude a soupy yellow

glow. VEPs are probably my least favourite Southern EMUs - they're so very boring - but I have to admit that No 3449 rides a lot more smoothly than an EPB.

The last time I used Gillingham station I was on my way to Katmandu - I'll explain some other time the quickest route from the Medway towns to Nepal - but I'd never travelled over the section from Gillingham to Canterbury before, so the four tracks as far as Newington, the Cerestar Gruppo Ferazzi bogie tankers at Sittingbourne, the sea cranes to the north at the mouth of the Medway, and a handsome rather Norman-looking half-timbered farmhouse were all new to me.

haps by now was?) almost the last stronghold of this combination. Both East and West stations sport them, along with their attendant pre-Grouping boxes.

We walk through Canterbury, past crowds of Christmas shoppers doing their utmost to dispel any notion that cash and cashcards are in short supply, through the ancient West Gate, and up to the West station, where we are back on familiar ground. My first journey here was in Southern Railway days, just after the war, from Minster to Ashford, hauled by an 'L' Class 4-4-0. My father and I travelled in a brand new Bulleid corridor 3rd, one of those of part corridor, part saloon layout, of the type preserved and working on the Swanage Railway. I thought it an attractive vehicle with its comfortable seats and big picture windows.

Today both platforms are thronged with customers. The barriers across the main road at the London end of the station are lowered, the signal arm swings up, and a couple of CEPs ease in. No soon-

Faversham boasts a four-platform station with lots of shapely iron railings and decorative awning supports, and we arrive there at 14.13. Time for a cup of tea and a piece of bread pudding in the buffet, manned by two ladies who are kept busy with a succession of customers.

An announcement informing us that our connection for Canterbury East had just left Sittingbourne and would be arriving at 14.33 is slightly optimistic, by 2 minutes, 50 seconds to be precise. It consists of 4VEP No 3492 and 4CEP No 1574. Once again the window cleaner is in dire need of a new chamois leather.

The 13 minute ride to Canterbury takes us past oast houses, hop fields and a couple of stone churches, with a fine view of the cathedral as we cross the line from Canterbury West on the outskirts of the city.

If you are a connoisseur of semaphore signals and the third rail then hurry to Canterbury for it is (per-

er have they departed under the big signal box which spans both tracks (there used to be four) for Minster and Ramsgate than the London train pulls in.

Just my luck, a couple of VEPs. I let the crowds squeeze into the front and find a compartment to myself in the rear of coach No 3496. Its windows are not as big and handsome as those on Bulleid steam stock, and, yes, they are, of course, dirty. Why does the Eastern Section allow it? It's very bad public relations.

Never mind, it's not so bad that I can't actually see out, and off we go along perhaps the most attractive stretch of railway in Kent, threading through the gentle and picturesque Stour Valley. Three stations of typical South Eastern Railway design, each with its own box and semaphore signals, serve the picture-book villages of Chartham, Chilham and Wye.

A buffet trolley plus attendant joins the lady guard at Ashford. They remain deep in conversation for nearly the entire 38-minute journey to Tonbridge, except for the stops at Pluckley, Headcorn, Staplehurst, Marden and Paddock Wood, so that I despair of ever getting any tea, but I do, just we pull into Tonbridge beside a long rake of bogie passenger brakes adorned in a variety of liveries. I once travelled this absolutely straight stretch behind a 'Schools' at the height of the hay fever season and sneezed all the way; perhaps it had something to do with the hops.

We stop only a matter of seconds at Tonbridge before we are off, swinging away from the original

SER main line to Redhill, and start the long climb up through the North Downs, past a girl lunging her grey horse round and round, followed by a golf course under construction - sign of the times - and then into Sevenoaks Tunnel, emerging into the gathering dusk to pull up alongside a Thameslink Class '319' bound for Bedford. I still can't quite get over the notion of being able to board an electric train in Kent, and get out of it half way up the Midland main line to Derby.

Lights are twinkling on the slopes of the North Downs as we climb through Dunton Green and plunge into Polhill Tunnel, coming out amongst the inter-war semi-detacheds of Chelsfield. The glows of the Honda garage at Orpington reflect in the windows of numerous 4EPBs stabled in the platforms and sidings.

Narrow-bodied No 33208 has charge of a ballast train at Hither Green where work is well under way in connection with Channel Tunnel traffic. Despite lack of government finance and various delays imposed upon BR, one cannot but be aware of preparations for the great day when, not Luton or Bedford, but Paris, Brussels and eventually all manner of exotic destinations will be one train ride away from Kent.

I never fail to respond to the excitement of the approach to a London terminus at night - the signals shining along the many tracks, trains rushing past in the opposite direction with glimpses of those inside, the lights from the tall office blocks and flats all around, an illuminated church spire, a sudden crossing of a bridge with traffic passing beneath and street lamps and glowing neon shop signs. The elevated tracks leading to London Bridge have all this and more, for many of the great landmarks of the capital come into view as the train nears the City - Tower Bridge, St Paul's, the Telecom Tower and Richard Rogers's wonderful Lloyds building dotted with purple, pink, yellow and green lights.

The evening star, Venus, is a bright pinpoint above the tower blocks to the west against the last red glow of the now vanished sun as we negotiate Borough Junction past a jumbled roofscape which seems hardly to have changed in nigh on 50 years, and draw into Waterloo East at 16.54.

My final train of the day is standing at platform 11 in the South Western station, the 17.32 Network Express to Weymouth. I board the leading unit, 'Wessex Electric' No 2408 *County of Dorset*, find a seat with a table in the front carriage, claim it, and then walk to the end of the platform to watch the 17.15 to Exeter depart behind a '47', releasing one of the few remaining Class '50s', which then backs down on to the 18.16 to Salisbury.

Suddenly a rocket, then another, shoot into the sky above the station roof and explode into glorious starbursts of gold and purple. The driver of the '50' leans out of his window, grins and yells something I can't quite catch, drowned in the roar of his engine.

We leave on time, and as we glide through Surbiton a ticket collector appears, the first such encounter since my journey on Thameslink from Farringdon to Peckham Rye; are the finances of the Eastern Section in such a parlous state that it can afford neither up-to-date rolling-stock, nor window cleaners and ticket collectors? Perhaps they'd be better if it had more of the latter. The 'Wessex Electrics' are the flagships of Network SouthEast and I take great delight that they are my local trains. They are beautiful to look at and a delight to ride in.

A digital clock on Basingstoke station given to flights of fancy shows 18.71 as we rush through. Rows of Class '47s', a Class '37' and a '60' (there must have been some '33s' too) are at rest in the yard at Eastleigh. Toys R Us opposite Southampton station looks more like a warehouse than a proper toy shop, and the *Canberra* is still in dock, floodlit with smoke drifting from her funnels - no doubt she will be gone before the morning.

We come to a halt in the depths of the New Forest and eventually pull into Brockenhurst station some 12 minutes down, being diverted most unusually into the up loop platform, the other three all being occupied, the down fast by two-car rail-cleaning unit No 930004, a 4SUB conversion. It got in our way, whatever it was. We arrive at Bournemouth at 19.26 and are off again at 19.29, much faster than in the days when '33s' had to be attached.

Journey's end for me comes at Wareham at 19.49. Signalman Bob's Vauxhall Astra is parked in the yard - rather grandly renamed 'Wareham Depot' since electrification - so I pop into his box, complete with its brown lino which someone ought to preserve one day, roaring fire, rows of gleaming levers and a calendar kindly donated by a local builders merchants featuring the Chairman's niece wearing a very nice smile.

'Funny, every train's been on time today until yours,' he says accusingly, as though it was my fault, so I explain that it was all No 930004's.

Although the last semaphore signal disappeared from the Wareham area at the time of electrification (the nearest one is on the Hamworthy branch) Steam Age technology still controls the 'Wessex Electrics' quite satisfactorily, although none of the signalmen are happy with the gateless, automatically-signalled pedestrian crossing at the end of the platforms; nor indeed are the local people or the council. The old gates controlled by signalmen were replaced on the grounds of cost saving - what a miserly, penny-pinching attitude the Thatcher administration had towards our splendid railway system.

Never mind, I had a lovely day out, and all for a fiver.

Type	Unit numbers	In service	Renumbered		Withdrawn
4LAV	1921-53	1931/2	2921-53	1937	1968-9
4LAV	2954-55	1940			1968
6PUL	2001-20	1932	3001-20	1937	1964-6
6CIT	2041-43*	1932	3041-43	1937	1964-6

* reformed as 6PULs in 1946

Type	Unit numbers	In service	Renumbered		Withdrawn
5BEL	2051-53	1932	3051-53	1937	1972
2NOL	1813-90	1934-6			1956-9
6PAN	2021-37	1935	3021-37	1937	1964-6
2BIL	1891-1900	1935	2001-10	1937	1967-9
2BIL	1901-20, 1954-71	1936	2011-48	1937	1968-70
2BIL	2049-2116	1937			1969-70
2BIL	2117-52	1938			1969-70
4COR	3101-29	1937			1970-72
4COR	3130-55	1938			1970-72
6COR*	3041-50	1967			1968

* Stop-gap Eastern Section units formed from former 6PUL/6PANs

Type	Unit numbers	In service	Renumbered		Withdrawn
4RES	3054-72	1937	Reformed 1946/64		1970-72
4BUF	3073-85	1938			1970
2HAL	2601-92	1939			1969-71
2HAL	2693-99	1948			1969-71
2HAL	2700	1955			1968
2HAP/414*	6001-42	1957/8	4201	1988	1982-
2HAP/414*	6043-6105	1958/9	4301-22	1988	1982-
2HAP/414*	6106-46	1961	4301-22	1988	1982-

* Some 2HAPs reformed 1977 as 2SAPs, many later reformed 1982 as 4CAPs

Type	Unit numbers	In service	Renumbered		Withdrawn
4CAP/413	3201-03, 3301-11	1982 (see above)			
4CEP/411	7101-04 (7102 disbanded)	1956	1503/4/2	1979	
4CEP/411	7105-7211	1958-63	1506-1621 2302-04	1979-84	
4BEP/412	7001-02	1956	1501/5	1979	
4BEP/412	7003-22	1958-63	1506-1621, 2302-04	1979-84	
4BEP/412	2301-07	1982*			

* Rebuilt from 7003-22/7105-7211 series

Type	Unit numbers	In service	Renumbered		Withdrawn
4CIG/421	7301-36	1964/5	*		
4CIG/421	7337-66	1970	*		
4CIG/421	7367-7437	1971/2	*		

* CIGs have been renumbered on more than one occasion into various sub-groups and can presently be found in the 11xx, 12xx, 13xx, 17xx and 18xx series

Type	Unit numbers	In service	Renumbered		Withdrawn
4BIG/422	7031-48	1964/5	2101-12, 2203-10	1988	
4BIG/422	7049-58	1970	2101-12, 2203-10	1988	
4REP/431	3001-11	1967	2001-11	1988	1988-91
4REP/431	3012-15	1974	2012-15	1988	1988-91

* In their last years the REPs saw several transformations; the final two units, renumbered 1901/4, worked spasmodically until early 1992

Type	Unit numbers	In service	Renumbered		Withdrawn
4TC/438	401-28	1966/7	8101-28	1988	1988-91
3TC*	429-31	1967	8129-31	1988	1988-91

* became 4TC in 1974

Type	Unit numbers	In service	Renumbered		Withdrawn
4TC/438	432-34	1974	1832-34	1988	1988-91

* The last two 4TCs, Nos 410/17, were formed in the autumn of 1991 into 'Premier Charter' units, repainted in 'Rail blue' and remain in service

Type	Unit numbers	In service	Renumbered	
4VEP/423	7701-20	1967	3001-20	1988
4VEP/423	7721-55	1967	3021-55	1988
4VEP/423	7756-7815	1968-70	3056-3115	1988
4VEP/423	7816-94	1972-4	3116-94	1988
5WES/442	2401-24	1987-9	'Wessex Electrics'	
319/0	319001-60	1987-8	'Thameslink'	
319/1	319161-86	1991	'Thameslink'	

Type and No	Built	Carriage Nos	Location
2BIL No 2090*	1937	10656, 12123	Brighton
4COR No 3142	1937	11161, 10096, 11825, 11201	St Leonards
4COR No 3131	1937	11179	National Railway Museum
6PUL/4COR No 3159	1932	11773	Swanage Railway
4COR No 3135	1937	11187	Nene Valley Railway
4BUF No 3084	1937	12613	Nene Valley Railway
6PUL No 3017	1932	'Ruth'	VSOE Stewarts Lane
6PUL No 3012	1932	'Bertha'	Bluebell Railway

* This is the only complete unit which is regularly seen at work on the third rail, although the Southern Electric Group is restoring its 4COR to this end.

In addition, all 15 of the 'Brighton Belle' Pullmans are still in existence, in various states of repair. None operates as a multiple unit but two, 'Audrey' and 'Vera', form part of the VSOE Pullman train and are still regularly electrically hauled.

Southern Region Class '71' Bo-Bo locomotive No E5001, built at Doncaster in 1958, is also preserved as part of the National Collection, and since the summer of 1992 has been passed for main-line running.